Praise For Conversations of a Watchman

"I will stand upon my watch, and set me upon the tower, and will watch to see what he will say unto me, and what I shall answer when I am reproved." Habakkuk 2:1 (KJV)

Minister Karla Allen is a true watchman that displays a genuine and intimate relationship with God. To anyone reading *Conversations of a Watchman*, digest it, meditate on it, and watch your life be transformed.

~First Lady A. Smith

"This is not some ordinary prayer book to read once and put on your shelf. *Conversations of a Watchman* is an indispensable guide that should be in every intercessor's and believer's library. Noted intercessor and author, K. E. Allen, has done an outstanding job in presenting to us how to advance the Kingdom of God through prayer. *Conversations of a Watchman* is highly recommended for those who desire to know the heart-beat of God."

Paulette Harper Johnson
Award winning author of *Completely Whole* and *That Was Then, This Is Now*

"Once in a while, new ground is broken and new territory is taken by the Kingdom of God. For this to happen, a fresh sound must be released, and a new voice must be heard. This is such a sound, and such a voice. I found *Conversations of a Watchman* to be a truly revelatory, Biblically sound, inspirational and empowering workbook. It is not meant simply to be read and put away. It is meant to be a daily guide and companion to encourage you in your daily prayer life. It will truly equip you to frame your world according to God's design and take new territory. Karla Allen has a crystal clear prophetic voice that is fresh, accurate, and anointed by the Spirit of God."

~**Apostle Bheki V. Gamedze**
Founding Senior Pastor of New Africa Gateway Church
Midrand, South Africa
President of the Hope International Apostolic Network

"I have had the honor of knowing Karla for over 26 years, and I can say from first-hand experience that she practices what she preaches. Karla's insight into the spirit realm through the vehicle of prayer is one that I, myself, have come to lean upon in various seasons of my life. You are about to be challenged, confronted, and catapulted into another dimension of understanding the will of God for your own prayer life. Embrace the principles set forth in this literary gem. You will never be the same."

Dr. Judith McAllister
President–International Music Department
COGIC

"What's BIG?" you ask. *Conversations of a Watchman* is both BIG and POWERFUL!

This book is one that every intercessor, prayer ministry, leadership team, and believer NEEDS in their arsenal. Because the enemy of our souls is strategic in his attack against us, we, as believers, must gain strategies to effectively combat the powers of darkness by learning to wield the God given weapon we have in prayer and intercession. If you are tired of praying and getting no results — seeing little or no change in your situation, then this book is for you. If you have a desire or feel the Lord calling you to a life of prayer or to a deeper level of prayer, then this book is for you.

As you read *Conversations of a Watchman*, you will be encouraged and stirred in your spirit to pray. By applying the practical principles within this book, you will see change in every area of your life. In your reading, you will glean from the revelation God has given to Author, K. E. Allen, and see breakthrough in every area of your life! As you read, you will learn to pray the heart and mind of God and take authority over the enemy. This mighty woman of God has an anointing to pray and get results. Reserve your copy today!

~Dasha Moore
The Moore Music Group Recording Artist

The ability to communicate effectively is the cornerstone of sustaining any relationship, and there is no relationship more significant than the relationship you have with God. In this day and time when the world's system of governance is failing, when global economic pressures impact your personal financial decisions, and when fear is the weapon of choice used by the enemy to disconnect you from the promises of God, your ability to speak to and hear from God clearly has never been more important. Allen will not only teach you "what" to pray, but will also teach you "how" to pray through Holy Spirit inspired examples of personal prayers, corporate prayers, and practical application exercises. *Conversations of a Watchman* by K. E. Allen is a must-have weapon in the spiritual arsenal of anyone looking to pattern their lives according to the Word of God by developing and sustaining an intimate "conversation" with Him.

~**Jamila Chambers,**
Life Coach and Founder of the Dream Studio
"Create a Life without Limits"

Conversations of a Watchman

Prayers to Frame Your Prophetic Destiny

K. E. Allen

Foreword by
Jackie Seeno

Published by Fresh Reign
P.O. Box 1091
Oakley, CA 94561

email: customercare@freshreign.com
website: www. freshreign.com
facebook: www.facebook.com/FreshReignPublishing
Twitter: @ fresh_reign
Printed in the United States of America

All rights reserved. No part of this publication may be reproduced, stored in a retrieval system, or transmitted in any form or by any means — for example, electronic, photocopy, and recording — without the prior written permission of the publisher. The only exception is brief quotations in printed reviews.

All Scripture quotations are taken from the *King James Version* of the *Holy Bible*.

Copyright © 2012 Karla E. Allen
All rights reserved

Library of Congress Catalog Card Number: 1-782783161

ISBN 978-0-9854480-0-4 (pbk)
ISBN 978-0-9854480-1-1 (ebk)

Dedication

This book is dedicated:

To my Heavenly Father, Jesus Christ, and the Holy Spirit– You are my secret hiding place.

To my grandparents, Peter and Mary Williams, and my parents, Charles Allen, Annie Lee and Richmond Turner, because of you I am. I am eternally grateful for the spiritual inheritance and legacy that you have imparted to me. I cannot wait until we are all together again. *To the countless intercessors,* who lay their lives down daily to see the heart of the Father accomplished, I pray that God will give you strength from His sanctuary.

To my sister, Kimberly, who for so many years, I longed to be. Your friendship, love, and support mean the world to me as your little sister. Thank you for being my second pair of eyes.

To my brother, Kruig, you have always been a big brother in every sense of the word. Thank you for taking care of Kim and me.

To my brother, Kevin, thank you for helping me gain the title of Coach K~. You taught me everything I know about being an exceptional basketball coach. Your practical wisdom has become spiritual wisdom.

To my nieces and nephews — Teddy, Genesis, Lauren, Ryan, Xavia, Jillian, Brittany, Mina, Ellah, Livee, Christian, C.J., Julian Alexander, Jaylen Austin, Devon, Brooklyn, Rashad, Maja, Timothy Jr., and Kayla — I challenge you to continue the spiritual legacy that you have been given.

Acknowledgments

It is amazing how a dream is conceived and developed over time, to become a living entity. Watching my God-idea mature into a living work would have never occurred without a community of people God sent and God used to be of assistance.

To my family by birth and choice, Regina Allen, Antoina Rivera-Grier, Denise Nickolas, Patricia Nickolas, Za' Nia Hanif, Danielle Williams, Dale Waggoner-Bolden, Jerone and Cynthia Williams, Peter and Jean Williams, Javen Williams, Janine Williams, Lerone and Aries Williams, Jason Williams, Benecia Williams, Marilyn Foxall, Barry and Latonya Thomas, Damia, Aunt Lillie B. Ransom and family, Aunt Johnnie Ayers and family, Uncle John and Aunt Mossie and family, Aunt Alice Boyer and family, Aunt Zelma Crowder and family, Aunt Helen Moultrie and family, the Prosser family, all of my Texas family, the Word family, the Herman family, the Matthews Family, the Neal family, Dad and Mom Moore, thank you for loving me.

To my inner circle of prophetic friends, Jackie Seeno, Dasha and Timothy Moore, Sr., Carl and Dorcas Cunningham, Brenda and Lloyd Walker, Sr., and Karla Torres and family, God only knows the countless tears and prayers offered on my behalf. May God hide you in the secret place of His tabernacle. May the Blood of Christ protect you, your loved ones, and those connected to you. Thank you for your insight, encouragement, and love.

To Bishop Smith, your fathering spirit brought me to a place where I could once again fulfill the call of God on my life. *To Lady Adrienne*, thank you for your graciousness and thoughtfulness. It is an honor to serve a man and a woman of God, whose hearts are perfect toward the only True and Living God. *To Sylvia, Sara, and Crystal*, I love you.

To Kimra, your unique, prophetic, and artistic gift helped bring to life, in picture form, what was in my heart.

To my prayer network, in the final stages of this project, your prayers were the wind beneath my wings. May God Himself reward you.

To Devin, may God give you the desires of your heart. May God breathe on everything you put your hands to do. May He equip you for the days ahead and surround you with His goodness.

To my Oral Roberts' University Crew, Darin and Judith McAllister, Tammy Davis, Karen Conway, Keith Childress, Christie Taylor, Margaret Bell, Mark and Da'dra Greathouse, Bheki and Shari Gamedze, David and Evangeline Smith, Steve Lyman, Corrine Conway, and Sandra Conway, your constant truth and love have helped develop me throughout the years. I thank God for you. May God continue to make us what we ought to be.

To Erica, you were my second wind in the last quarter. May God grant you a fresh impartation of grace.

To my Neighborhood and Shekinah family: Kirk and Denise Davis, Lane and Toyea Hawkins, James Adams, Thomas Taper the III, the Gillette family, the Morris family, the Davis family, the George family, the Hall family, the Pope family, Maude Coleman, Allan and Roxanne Roberts, Alice Martin Dickson-Porter, Helanie Robinson, Vincent and Regina Wilson, Toni Powell, and Bonita Melendez, I thank God for His faithfulness to us.

To my NBC family: the Music and Worship Arts team and your children, the Production team, the Prayer team, Executive Services, the Culinary team, the Parking Lot team, the Administrative Staff, the Clergy, the Servant Leaders and their Volunteers, and my entire church family, thank you for allowing me to serve with you.

To my friends in the ministry: Dallas and Heather Dawson, Gail Knowles, Tamara and Morgan Pacini, Darren and Radha Richmond, Paul and Stephanie Jackson, Lonnie and Denise Smith, Rufus and Jamila Chambers, Doris and Joey Bumpus Sr., Linda and Garrick Mallory, Oscar and Carol Jones, Will and J.C. Humphrey, Debra Porter, Tracy Lewis, Ronnel and Erica Benjamin, Dave and Cassandra Daniels, Ray and Tacoma Hagler, Anthony and Ornicia Lowe, Karen Gaskin, Cyrenius and

Edwina Forh, Dave and Danielle Robinson, Ron and Mildred Hill, Rucker and Candace Johnson, Paulette Harper Johnson, Tamela Jones, Genea Brice, Chee Chee Chillers, Aaron and Nashone Holmes, Gina Fiame, Kamilah Tom, and Nick Burse, thank you for allowing God to use you in my spiritual maturity.

Table of Contents

Foreword   *18*

PREFACE

The Call   *20*

PROLOGUE

Who is the Watchman?   *24*

A Word to the Watchman   *26*

INTRODUCTION

Keys to Framing Your Prophetic Destiny   *28*

CHAPTER ONE

Keys to Framing Your Prophetic Destiny: The Holy Spirit   *30*

CHAPTER TWO

Keys to Framing Your Prophetic Destiny: The Word of God   *32*

CHAPTER THREE

Keys to Framing Your Prophetic Destiny: The Light of God   *35*

CHAPTER FOUR

Keys to Framing Your Prophetic Destiny: Proclaiming   *38*

CHAPTER FIVE

Practical Application   41

ODE TO ISRAEL

Prayer for the Peace of Jerusalem   47

THE FIRST WATCH

The Love of God   52

The Mind of Christ   56

Godly Wisdom and Discernment   58

Psalm 18   60

My Daily Bread   64

Mending Breaches   68

Repositioning   72

A Fresh Confession   74

Committing Your Friendships to God   78

God's Provision   80

Father, Grant Me a Husband   82

God's Divine Order   86

THE SECOND WATCH

Draw Me   92

A Song of Solomon   94

Your Character	98
Eat Your Portion	104
A Place by Me	106
Arise and Shine	110
Be Restored	112
The Breeze of My Spirit	114
A Time of Refreshing	116
Generational Blessings	118
The Day of Release	120
The Hand of the Lord	122
An Open Gate	126
Hear, Listen, and Obey	128
I Will Hear, Listen, and Obey	129
The Promise of a River	132
Timing and Destiny	134

THE THIRD WATCH

A Word to California	138
A Prayer for California	139
Breakthrough Prayer	142
Persistent Prayer	148

The Deliverance Decree	*150*
Isaiah 42	*154*
Standing in the Gap	*158*
Restoring the Foundations of Righteousness	*162*
Digging the Wells of Revival	*166*
A Watchman's Prayer for the Ministry	*168*
A Watchman's Prayer for Pastors	*172*
The Enemy's Strategy — Conspiracies	*176*
A Prayer Against Conspiracies	*177*
Fan the Flames to Harvest the Souls	*180*

Foreword

When I met Karla Allen in the summer of 2007, the Lord revealed to me the special anointing "to watch" that is upon her life. Since that time, I have had the honor of walking with Karla, cultivating a dear friendship with her; along with watching and learning from her intimate–passionate relationship with God.

It is a privilege to be alive during this exciting and critical season in Earth's history. God is moving in and through His creation in profound, manifest ways and is releasing powerful revelation to bring His bride to a place of maturity. In this season, prophetic voices can often be heard saying, "God is doing a new thing!" Indeed, God is doing new things, but much of what we perceive to be the new thing is often the restoration of an old, ancient thing that has been forgotten that it looks "new" when it appears in its full restoration!

This generation is the Lord's restoration creation and in this season of restitution, God is reinstating the anointing of the Watchman to His Church. The individual Watchman's role varies in scope and sphere, but the primary functions of this prophetic-protective anointing are to watch, guard, hedge, and protect. *Isaiah 21:6* illustrates the mandate of the Watchman well: *"Go, set a watchman, let him declare what he seeth."* Out of intimate fellowship, the Holy Spirit releases revelation to the Watchman, who through Spirit-led strategic intercession can dismantle and neutralize the fiery onslaughts of the enemy.

As we learn to develop and activate the Watchman's anointing, we will be able to fulfill the dominion mandate of *Genesis 1:26-28* and become operative in our identity as kings and priests unto God *(Revelations. 5:10)*. It is from this position that we will truly begin to take territory, advance the Kingdom, and occupy every sphere of influence in the Earth realm until He returns!

Karla birthed *Conversations of a Watchman* in the secret place of deep and loving communion with our Father. As a committed, consistent, disciplined, and passionate intercessor, Karla allows us to enter into her prayer closet and private watches with the Lord. We can all learn from the prophetic and intercessory anointing on her life.

It is my prayer that God will breathe and blow fresh wind as you read the pages of this book, causing you to have a transformative encounter with Him! May the God of Abraham, Isaac, and Jacob open your spirit-womb and impregnate you with the passion, fire, and desire to engage the Spirit realm through prayer and intercession. Finally, may the anointing of the Watchman awaken within you to empower you to advance His Kingdom in Earth as it is in Heaven!

Prophetess Jackie Seeno

Preface

The Call

As you read this section, take time to prayerfully answer the questions.

WILL YOU ANSWER THE CALL TO INTERCEDE FOR OTHERS?

There are times in life when one encounters God in such tangible ways that it becomes physically overwhelming to the senses. I still remember it like it was yesterday — the moment I first experienced God's hand upon my life. This particular moment was different from times past. During my second year at Oral Roberts University, the Spirit of God visited me in an unusual way. I can only describe it as being cloaked with a robe that weighed more than I could carry. Throughout that period, I would try to eat and socialize with others like a normal 19-year-old student. However, the spirit of intercession would overwhelm me and I would run across campus weeping. What a foolish site I must have been.

During those times, I would run back to my room and cry out to God and pray in the spirit until I was relieved of the overpowering burden lodged in the center of my chest. As I often recant that period in my life to others, I always say, "I fasted more days than I ate." When I look back on that time, I realize God Himself was forming me into His intercessor.

Some say I have an anointing to pray and fast. The truth is the desire for God's presence, His will, and purpose often creates a spiritual desperation no natural food can satisfy. Seeing the will of God accomplished is true fulfillment.

By applying the principles of the Word of God regarding fasting and intercession, I have witnessed the reversal of court decisions, dramatic transformation of individuals, miraculous healings, and the restoration of family members.

It is God's desire to use man to accomplish His will in the Earth. Throughout the scriptures God uses ordinary people to accomplish extraordinary feats through intercession and fasting. It is only by His grace, through faith, and the empowerment of the Holy Spirit that believers accomplish anything, including interceding and fasting on the behalf of others.

Think about these few scriptural examples:

In Scripture, the intercession of Moses convinced God not to destroy the people of Israel *(Numbers 14:11-21)*.

WILL YOU CONVINCE GOD TO SHOW MERCY AS MOSES DID?

Esther, after organizing three days of fasting and intercession, delivered the Jewish nation from the plot of Haman — a plot that would have annihilated the entire Jewish race *(Esther 4:16)*.

WILL YOU PRAY FOR YOUR NATION TO EXPERIENCE TRUE DELIVERANCE?

The Scriptures also mention Anna, who for 84 years worshipped the Lord with continual fasting and praying until the birth of Christ *(Luke 2:21-38)*.

HOW LONG WILL YOU INTERCEDE TO SEE CHRIST BORN IN OTHERS?

These are powerful examples. Even so, the ultimate act of intercession was Jesus' death, burial, and resurrection from the dead. Christ's altruistic act empowers the believer to live an overcoming life. He has proven to be the Chief Intercessor who ever-lives to make intercession for us (*Hebrews 7:25*).

Engaging in the selfless act of intercession displays the characteristics of Christ, who is merciful and kind. He shows mercy to a thousand generations. Therefore, He is constantly looking for someone to demonstrate His personality and act as a bridge between Him and mankind.

God desires and chooses people who will build a wall of justice and institute His Kingdom rule on Earth as it is in heaven. He desires people who will reinforce His purposes. He desires someone who will be persistent to establish His heart in the Earth.

God desires hedge builders and gap fillers. ***He is calling*** for people willing to sacrifice their lives to preserve a person, a business, a community, a city, a region, a country, or a nation.

In *Numbers 16*, the Scriptures record: when the sons of Korah came against Moses, God sent a plague among the people as judgment. The Bible says Aaron lit the censer, made amends for the people, and stood between the living and the dead. His act of intercession stopped the plague (*Numbers 16: 1-50*).

As one intercedes according to the heart of God, the words spoken impede the strategies of the enemy and frame God's prophetic destiny.

WHOSE DESTINY WILL YOU REVOLUTIONIZE THROUGH INTERCESSION?

Prologue

Who is the Watchman?

The watchman is responsible for framing prophetic destiny spoken by the council of God. The watchman's anointing allows one to perceive accurately the enemy approaching from a distance to warn the people of God of the plots and plans of the enemy *(Ezekiel 33:1-6)*.

Conversely, when introduced to Christ, believers usually gain knowledge of one dimension or one kind of prayer — "the prayer of petition." This type of prayer involves asking the Father for personal needs and desires. Unfortunately, because of insufficient training, countless believers fail in this initial level of prayer and lose the desire or interest before discovering the true, hidden treasures found in prayer. Discerning the extent by which believers can communicate with the Father creates an inward hunger and thirst to know Him more.

As one matures and develops a disciplined prayer life, prayer becomes a conversation based on God's covenant, God's heart, God's mind, and God's purpose. God and His purpose are the center and focus of every dialogue. Essentially, prayer is an exchange of ideas about His purpose pertaining to one's family, ministry, business, community, and nation. This is the key to successful prayer — exchanging self generated thoughts for God's thoughts. When one prays apart from God's desires, there is no guarantee of answered prayers. The assurance comes when one's desires align with His. Asking according to His will cultivates the confidence that He hears, He answers *(1 John 5:14-15),* and He is faithful. Understanding God's authenticity facilitates a deeper level of conversation based on relationship.

The depth of one's conversation depends on the depth of the relationship. The more intimately one knows a person, the deeper the conversation. Closeness automatically creates an atmosphere for a transparent, authentic exchange. Intimate conversation allows face-to-face interactions in which nothing is hidden. This kind of exchange allows one to know the secret place of another's heart well enough to speak for them. This is the watchman.

In other words, the watchman relies on his **intimate relationship** with God to preserve his sensitivity in spiritual warfare. In essence, the requisite for the watchman maintaining his prophetic precision is standing in the presence of God waiting for instruction *(Habakkuk 2:1-2).*

The watchman surrounds himself with other prophetic gifts, such as gatekeepers. Gatekeepers war at spiritual gates, to prevent the enemy from gaining entrance into the lives of individuals, families, ministries, businesses, communities, regions, states, countries, and nations. In a symphonic synergistic way, the gifts flow in concert to provide warning to the people of God by discerning the will of God and receiving intercessory strategy from the Holy Spirit to overcome an already defeated adversary.

A Word to the Watchman

__Word to the Watchman__ from the one whose...eyes run to and fro throughout the whole earth, to shew himself strong in the behalf of [them] whose heart [is] perfect toward him...(2 Chronicles 16:9).

While you are watching for Me, I am watching over you. Watch not on your own, but watch through My eyes that you may see clearly. I watch over My Word to perform it. Therefore, in your watching, speak the Word. I will perform and manifest the Word you speak.

This is the season and the time I will arise to establish and confirm what I have spoken. That which I have sworn, I will perform. Watch and wait to see what I will do. For this is the season of fulfillment. This is the season of manifestation.

Pressing is a part of the watching process, so be encouraged! Your regimented press will yield creative fruit others will enjoy.

INTRODUCTION

Keys to Framing Your Prophetic Destiny

In the beginning God created the heaven and the earth. And the earth was <u>without form</u>, and <u>void</u>; and <u>darkness [was] upon the face of the deep</u>. And the <u>Spirit of God moved</u> upon the face of the waters. And <u>God said</u>, Let there be light: and there was light. And <u>God saw</u> the light, that [it was] good: and <u>God divided</u> the light from the darkness. And <u>God called</u> the light Day, and the darkness he called Night. And the evening and the morning were the first day (Genesis 1:1-5).

Genesis 1 paints a picture of the Earth and the deep prior to creation. The Earth was without form. It was in a confused state. It was a wilderness and a place of chaos. The Earth was empty. The Earth had no frame or clear form. The Earth was void of organization and lacked the basic essentials to display an articulate image of itself. It lacked the ability to produce. It was a desolate place. In essence, the essential character of the Earth was not visible. Alongside of desolate Earth, existed the deep that was deficient of light. Both were entities operating outside of prophetic destiny. Nevertheless, the Earth was meant to be a conduit for man to carry out the purpose and plan of God, and a place of productivity. The water destined to be a source of refreshment, growth, and life.

As I describe the condition of the Earth and the deep, you may see yourself or certain aspects of your life or someone else's life in the same condition. If this is the case, we have to begin asking significant questions: How does one move from a place deficient of light? How does one move from a place of apathy and complacency? How does one move from a place of misery, and continual misfortune? How does a person learn to live in a state of divine prophetic destiny?

Over the next few pages we will explore, in short, the fundamental keys for moving from a place of frustration and lack into your prophetic destiny. Through your trust and confidence towards God, you must learn to cultivate an atmosphere for the Holy Spirit to manifest. Subsequently, under the inspiration of the Holy Spirit you must be able to speak the Word of God accurately.

The Word of God acts as a streetlight in the midst of your "moments of darkness" and allows you to see clearly the path God has designed for you. Ultimately, as you imitate the blueprint witnessed at creation, you release the creative power of the God of Creation, Elohim, for prophetic destiny.

CHAPTER ONE

Keys to Framing Your Prophetic Destiny: The Holy Spirit

...And the <u>Spirit of God moved</u> upon the face of the waters (Genesis 1:2)

The word "Spirit" used in *Genesis 1*, is the Hebrew word "rü'·akh." It is translated Wind, Breath, Mind, and Spirit of God. In essence, the Wind, Breath, Mind, and Spirit of God were moving on the face of the waters. The Spirit of God was manifesting the Glory of God and creating an atmosphere for the creative Word of God to operate.

In order for the world to witness the never-ending government of God, it is imperative to create an atmosphere of glory and discern what God desires to release. King David understood a key principle regarding unlocking the mysteries of the Kingdom of God. He reveals his secret *in Psalm 49:4, "I will incline mine ear to a parable: I will open my dark saying upon the harp."* The release of prayer and worship, based on God's Words, has the ability to shift atmospheres and create environments in which God is able to produce extraordinary, enduring results. In Scripture, prophesy is frequently accompanied by music. In fact, the absence of music and singing was associated with a place of captivity or bondage (*Psalm 137*).

The Apostle Paul understood this principle as well. Paul declares in *I Corinthians 14:15*, *"What is it then? I will pray with the Spirit and I will pray with the understanding also: I will sing with the Spirit and I will sing with the understanding also."* As you merge worship and intercession with the help of the Holy Spirit, He will reveal the wonders of His person. Worship and intercession released out of relationship empowers you to accurately release the Kingdom of God in Earth as it is in Heaven (*Matthew 6:10*).

When you have mastered this principle, it does not matter where you are in life because in the place of confusion, the *Breath of God* is waiting to impart peace and divine order. In the wilderness — the dry place, *the Spirit of God*, like rain filled clouds, is present to pour out the former and the latter rain to refresh. In your empty place, the *Mind of God* is there to express the fullness of God found in Christ Jesus. When you fail, the *Spirit of God* knows how to bring about a successful ending. When you fall short of producing an authentic image, the *Spirit of God* is revealing His likeness. When the vision has not manifested, the *Spirit of God* imparts patience to finish. When the basic necessities are lacking, the *Spirit of God* comes with an abundant supply. In the midst of the *Wind, Breath, Mind,* and *Spirit of God,* you only need faith reminiscent of the Centurion man who said to Jesus in *Matthew 8:8, "speak the word only…"*

Chapter Two

Keys to Framing Your Prophetic Destiny: The Word of God

And God said, Let there be... (Genesis 1:3)

*Through faith we understand that the worlds were **<u>framed</u>** by the word of God, so that things which are seen were not made of things which do appear (Hebrews 11:3).*

The Word "framed" is "kä-tär-tē'-zō" in the Greek. It is interpreted to render fit, to mend what is broken, to equip, to arrange, to strengthen, to perfect, to restore to harmony, to join perfectly together, to imagine, to give utterance, and to adapt for a particular purpose. The process of framing begins with a God-breathed idea. The idea expands and develops in your God given imagination. Once the idea is completely enlarged, the Holy Spirit stirs within you a divine utterance to release your destiny. Essentially, through the power contained in the words you speak, you bring God-motivated dreams to a place of authenticity. **If the Word of God is able to**

frame the worlds, the Word of God is able to arrange your destiny. In the end, <u>by faith,</u> you see that which is not visible, yet exists in the invisible realm, made evident by the Word of God.

> *God, who at sundry times and in divers manners spake in time past unto the fathers by the prophets, Hath in these last days spoken unto us by [his] Son, whom he hath appointed heir of all things, <u>by whom also he made the worlds</u>; Who being the brightness of [his] glory, and the express image of his person, and <u>upholding all things by the word of his power</u>, when he had by himself purged our sins, sat down on the right hand of the Majesty on high; (Hebrews 1: 1-3)*

Not only does the Word of God position you to live your destiny, it will sustain your future. **God keeps everything from failing by the authority that exists in His Word.** God is obligated to accomplish His Word. If you know what God is saying, failure is impossible. The truth revealed in Genesis and Hebrews demonstrates to us that *whatever God speaks to has to respond.* All creation must act in response to its Creator — Elohim.

> *In the beginning was the Word, and the Word was with God, and the Word was God. The same was in the beginning with God. <u>All things were made by</u>*

him; and without him was not any thing made that was made. In him was life; and the life was the light of men (John 1:1-4).

The Life and the Light of your destiny is in the Word of Go

CHAPTER THREE

Keys to Framing Your Prophetic Destiny: The Light of God

...Let there be light... (Genesis 1:3)

The first thing God created out of the midst of chaos and darkness was light. The declaration of the promise and counsel of God illuminates and produces an environment for restoration and growth. It ultimately gives way to the ability to distinguish the purpose of God.

> *The entrance of thy words giveth light; it giveth understanding unto the simple (Psalm 119:130).*

> *Then spake Jesus again unto them, saying, I am the light of the world: he that followeth me shall not walk in darkness, but shall have the light of life (John 8:12).*

For with thee [is] the fountain of life: in thy light shall we see light (Psalm 36:9).

With Christ, Who is Light, there is restoration, provision, and prosperity. In His brightness, we can perceive, observe, discern, distinguish, see, and be seen.

Light Gives Way to Discernment.

God divided the light from the darkness... (Genesis 1:4)

For we preach not ourselves, but Christ Jesus the Lord; and ourselves your servants for Jesus' sake. For <u>God, who commanded the light to shine out of darkness</u>, hath shined in our hearts, to [give] the light of the knowledge of the glory of God in the face of Jesus Christ (2 Corinthians 4:5-6).

This then is the message which we have heard of him, and declare unto you, that <u>God is light</u>, and <u>in him is no darkness at all</u>. If we say that we have fellowship with him, and walk in darkness, we lie, and do not the truth: But if we <u>walk in the light, as he is in the light</u>, we have fellowship one with another, and the blood of Jesus Christ his Son cleanseth us from all sin (1 John 1:5-7).

The word "divided" used in *Genesis Chapter 1* is "badal" in the Hebrew. It is the same word used for sever and asunder. Therefore, when God divided the light from the darkness, He distinguished one from the other. This separation gave way to what God <u>called</u> the first Day.

When the Word of God enters into your circumstance, it enables you to identify with the divine will of God for your life. Once you become aware of the will of God, as a believer, you are authorized to proclaim His will in the Earth.

Chapter Four

Keys to Framing Your Prophetic Destiny: Proclaiming

God called the light Day...

And <u>God called</u> the light Day, and the darkness he called Night. And the evening and the morning were the first day (Genesis 1:5).

The word "called," used in *Genesis 1:5*, is "Ka'ra" meaning to proclaim. According to Webster's dictionary, "proclaim" means to announce insistently, proudly, or defiantly in writing or speech. "Proclaim" also means to declare, decree, or make known. God decreed and declared when He created the Heavens and the Earth. Likewise, as an imitator of God, you have to become a prophetic messenger and begin to proclaim and frame your ideal world by proclaiming, decreeing, and declaring the Word of God over your life and circumstances.

Invite the assistance of God through the creative ability that exists in the Word of God, the authoritative Name of Jesus Christ, and the prevailing Blood of the Lamb. Ask the Holy Spirit to give you understanding concerning God's plan for your life, so you can apply the spiritual principle found in *Romans 4:17* to every area of your life.

> *(As it is written, I have made thee a father of many nations,) before him whom he believed, [even]* <u>*God, who*</u> *quickeneth the dead, and* <u>*calleth those things which be not as though they were*</u> *(Romans 4:17).*

As a son or daughter of God, you have the same attributes as your Heavenly Father. You are a speaking spirit created in the likeness of God. Therefore, you must emulate your Father and manifest your prophetic destiny by speaking it into existence. Through the imaginative preeminence that exists in the Word of God, you must declare His will for your life in Earth as it is in Heaven.

If you are willing to allow the work of the Holy Spirit to shine the Light of the Word into every dark area of your life, this could be your first day to walk in God's divine plan for your life.

For I reckon that the sufferings of this present time [are] not worthy [to be compared] with the glory which shall be revealed in us (Romans. 8:18).

Chapter Five

Practical Application

As you decree and declare, there are foundational, scriptural principles necessary for successful application of this resource.

1. Pray to the Father as Jesus instructed his disciples to do in *Matthew 6:9*

After this manner therefore pray ye: Our Father which art in heaven, Hallowed be thy name.

2. Pray in the name of Jesus, based on the following scriptures: *John 14:13; John 14:1; John 15:16; John 16:23-26*

And whatsoever ye shall ask in my name, that will I do, that the Father may be glorified in the Son (John 14:13).

3. Pray in faith with a forgiving heart.
Therefore I say unto you, What things soever ye desire, when ye pray, believe that ye receive them,

and ye shall have them. And when ye stand praying, forgive, if ye have ought against any: that your Father also which is in heaven may forgive you your trespasses (Mark 11:24-25).

When you decree and declare, you are stating emphatically and authoritatively an order, directive, or command enforced by God's covenant promises. As you decree and declare the Word, two principles are in operation:

- By His own agreement**, God obligates Himself** to fulfill His promises *(Matthew 18:19-20).*
- When you exercise your God given authority through the Word, it **neutralizes the enemy** *(Matthew 16:19).*

The following is an example of praying or declaring the Word:

Sing unto the Lord a new song, and His praise from the end of the earth, ye that go down to the sea, and all that is therein; the isles, and the inhabitants thereof (Isaiah 42:10).

Prophetic Decree:

(A simple definition for a prophetic decree is communicating with inherent authority, by the leading of the Holy Spirit, the heart and mind of God at the opportune moment for maximum Kingdom results.)

> 1. *We sing unto the Lord a new song and His praise from our region. We sing a song in our region that has never been heard. The song that You give us shall pierce the darkness and open the windows, gates, and portals of heaven for the King of glory to come in perpetually.*
>
> Or
>
> 2. *We decree and declare that a new song and praise be released to the Lord from our region. We decree and declare that a song be released from our region that has never been heard. We decree and declare it will pierce the darkness and open the windows, gates, and portals of heaven for the King of Glory to come in perpetually.*

Use the scriptures referenced at the bottom of each prayer to help you begin to know what God is saying. Then, find additional scriptures. Take the time to look up the words in a Bible concordance, Bible dictionary, and regular dictionary for further understanding. As you read, be sensitive to the Holy Spirit. If a particular Word or phrase seems to stand out more than others, stop there and **ask the Holy Spirit** what He wants to reveal or say to you. This will assist you in writing your own prophetic decrees.

Take time to meditate on the words, phrases, or passages the Holy Spirit highlights to you. *To **meditate** simply means to think about the words, phrases, or passages continually and allow the Holy Spirit to speak to you further. You may recite the words, phrases, or passages repeatedly or picture them in your mind while praying in the Spirit.* The key is to place yourself in a position for the Father to speak to your heart.

The prayers in this book were derived from my intimate conversations with the Father. As you prayerfully decree, declare, and meditate on the prayers in this book, I pray you are stirred to develop deeper dimensions of conversational intimacy with Him. I challenge you to begin to *frame your prophetic destiny* through your own conversations with the Father in Jesus' name. Amen!

Ode to Israel

I have set watchmen upon thy walls, O Jerusalem, which shall never hold their peace day nor night: ye that make mention of the Lord, keep not silence, And give him no rest, till he establish, and till he make Jerusalem a praise in the earth (Isaiah 62:6-7).

Prayer for the Peace of Israel

Father, no one has ever found You to be a liar. You do not deceive or disappoint because Your very name is Faithful and True. You never go back on Your promises, and no one or nothing can undo what You have intended. Once You speak, Your Word is ratified.

Who is strong enough to invalidate Your Words? Your Word is the only Word worthy of a Name. It is the breath among the living and powerful in action. Israel is blessed and no one can nullify it.

You have forgiven Israel. You are with Israel, and the sound of Your voice is sounding as a trumpet in the midst of them. Israel is blessed. There is no incantation, deception, trick, or scheme against Israel that can prosper. Israel is blessed. There is no divination, witchcraft, nation, or false prophet that can supersede Your Word. Israel is blessed.

Father, Your eyes are on Israel, and Your face is toward her. Israel is the apple of Your eye. Where Israel dwells is beautiful because You have planted Israel like trees by waters. From Israel shall flow a source of refreshment to future generations, and the Kingdom of Israel shall be glorious.

Father, I declare Your Word: You will overcome those who oppose Israel. Blessed are those who bless Israel, and cursed is everyone that curses Israel.

I pray for the peace of Jerusalem. May all who love the Holy City flourish. I decree and declare peace reigns within the walls of Jerusalem, and wealth and riches are in her palaces.

To the mountains and hills, to the ravines and valleys, to the desolate lands, and forsaken cities I prophesy, "Oh Mountains of Israel shoot forth your branches and yield your fruit to Israel."

Father, remember Your covenant to Israel, whom You love, and turn to them. Till and sow Israel for Your divine purpose.

Rebuild the waste places, multiply, increase, and cause them to be fruitful. I declare that Israel's end will be greater than her beginning. Father, fortify the ruins and replant the desolate places of Your holy city.

> *"Oh that the salvation of Israel were come out of Zion! When God bringeth back the captivity of his people, Jacob shall rejoice, and Israel shall be glad." (Psalm 53:6)*

I seal this prayer in the name of Jesus the Christ. Amen.

Scripture References: *Hebrews 4:12; Numbers 23-25; Psalm 1*

PRAYERS TO FRAME YOUR PROPHETIC DESTINY
WORKSHEET

(This may be used as a guide to help you begin to frame your destiny.)

My personal Conversation with the Father regarding:

_____

Discover what the Word of God says about:

_____

Look up and write down the verses in the Bible that mention the word(s), phrase(s), or concept(s):

_____
_____

How are these word(s), phrase(s), or concept(s) applicable to you, your family, your church, your community, or your nation?

_____
_____

What do you want to say to the Father about what He has said?

_____
_____

Take a moment to meditate on the Word(s) that seem more pronounced to you as you read what God has to say. After meditating on what He has said, what do you hear the Holy Spirit speaking to your Heart? Take the Scriptures you found, along with what the Holy Spirit is speaking to your heart, and use them to change and frame your destiny:

_____
_____
_____

Prayer Quote

"Intercession is love on its knees in prayer for others."

~Bishop Tudor Bismark

Prayers to Frame Your Prophetic Destiny

The First Watch

The Love of God

Father, I thank You that the love of God is shed abroad in my heart by the Holy Spirit. Through the help of the Holy Spirit, I patiently endure in the spirit of kindness. Because of Your love at work in me, I counter envy and jealousy with the love of God and boast only in the Lord Jesus Christ. I resist pride, and I choose to walk in the spirit of humility.

Father, by Your grace, I humble myself and speak well of others' accomplishments. I submit myself to You and resist the temptation to boast. I demonstrate the fruit of Your Spirit in my life through joy, peace, longsuffering, gentleness, kindness, and meekness.

Because Your love is active in me, I will not lose heart. I will persevere through adversity, sickness, and pain — both mental and physical. Through the power of Your Love, I will pray for those who offend me. I will be slow to retaliate, slow to anger, and slow to penalize.

There is no agony in mature love. Your love completes and refines. Mature love throws out fear because fear has harsh consequences. Fear puts to flight, startles through strange occurrences, seizes with alarm, and causes hesitation. Therefore, I resist the spirit of fear, and I submit to Your love that I may have true affection for You and mankind.

Father, Your love provides relief. Your Love is sympathetic, helpful, affectionate, and gentle. Therefore, I stand firm against the idea of taking advantage of others. You have given all things that pertain to life and godliness. Therefore, I choose to focus on Your total provision and an unlimited supply. Father, my exertion and inspiration is for You alone because You are love.

I seal this prayer in the name of Jesus the Christ. Amen.

Scripture references*: I Corinthians 13; Romans 5:5*

Prayers to Frame your Prophetic Destiny
Worksheet

(This may be used as a guide to help you begin to frame your destiny.)

My personal Conversation with the Father regarding:

_____

Discover what the Word of God says about:

_____
_____
_____

Search out and write down the verses in the Bible that mention the word(s), phrase(s), or concept(s):

_____
_____
_____
_____

How are these word(s), phrase(s), or concept(s) applicable to you, your family, your church, your community, or your nation?

_____
_____
_____
_____
_____
_____
_____
_____

What do you want to say to the Father about what He has said?

___

Take a moment to meditate on the Word(s) that seem more pronounced to you as you read what God has to say. After meditating on what He has said, what do you hear the Holy Spirit speaking to your Heart? Take the Scriptures you found, along with what the Holy Spirit is speaking to your heart, and use them to change and frame your destiny:

___

The Mind of Christ

Father, let Your Holy Ghost fire purge me from every corrupt opinion, distorted principle, and false teaching. Let Your truth prevail in my heart and mind. I continually welcome Your truth in the innermost parts of myself. Allow Your truth to be the pervading force in every area of my life so that my thoughts, mind, words, and actions are free from ungodly affection, pretense, simulation, falsehood, and deceit.

I thank You that my passion is for Your presence and Your Word. I search after Your desires, Your heart, and Your glory.

I submit to the peace of God that passes understanding and resist the temptation to be easily irritated. I thank You that my mind is free to consider spiritual concepts. I refuse to give in to the temptation to consider or contemplate things contrary to Your plans and purposes. I reflect on beautiful things and meditate on Your Word in the day and night watches. I have the mind of Christ, so I can envision Your excellent design for my life.

I seal this prayer in the name of Jesus the Christ. Amen.

Scripture References: *Psalm 51:6; Philippians 4:7-8; Joshua 1:8; 1 Corinthians 2:16*

PRAYERS TO FRAME YOUR PROPHETIC DESTINY
WORKSHEET

(This may be used as a guide to help you begin to frame your destiny.)

My personal Conversation with the Father regarding:

___

Discover what the Word of God says about:

___

Look up and write down the verses in the Bible that mention the word(s), phrase(s), or concept(s):

___

___

How are these word(s), phrase(s), or concept(s) applicable to you, your family, your church, your community, or your nation?

___

___

What do you want to say to the Father about what He has said?

___

___

Take a moment to meditate on the Word(s) that seem more pronounced to you as you read what God has to say. After meditating on what He has said, what do you hear the Holy Spirit speaking to your Heart? Take the Scriptures you found, along with what the Holy Spirit is speaking to your heart, and use them to change and frame your destiny:

___

___

___

Godly Wisdom and Discernment

Blessed be the name of the Father forever and ever. You position and remove those in authority. You also give wisdom to the wise and knowledge to those with understanding. You reveal deep and secret things. You know what is in the darkness, and light dwells in You. I thank and praise You because You have given me the wisdom and capacity to understand the desires of Your heart.

Father, I pray for those in authority. I trust You will give me strategies to solve their problems. I declare, by Your grace, I effectively work with those in authority. I pray that I walk in spiritual discernment at all times. By the gift of discernment, I can separate and distinguish between Your Spirit and other spirits in all circumstances.

I thank You that I am well favored. I thank You that You bring me into favor, tender love, compassion, and loving kindness with those in authority, those with whom I work, and those who work for me.

I thank You that I operate in the spirit of wisdom, the spirit of revelation knowledge, the spirit of compassion, and the spirit of discernment that will empower me to walk with influential people in the seven mountains of culture. I thank You that I am apt in wisdom and competent to stand before all authority in the ability that I have in Christ Jesus.

I seal this prayer in the name of Jesus the Christ. Amen.

Scripture Reference: *Daniel 2:21; 1 John 1:5; 1 Timothy 2: 1-4; Proverbs 8:35; Proverbs 3:13-26*

PRAYERS TO FRAME YOUR PROPHETIC DESTINY
WORKSHEET

(This may be used as a guide to help you begin to frame your destiny.)

My personal Conversation with the Father regarding:

_____

Discover what the Word of God says about:

_____

Look up and write down the verses in the Bible that mention the word(s), phrase(s), or concept(s):

_____

_____

How are these word(s), phrase(s), or concept(s) applicable to you, your family, your church, your community, or your nation?

_____

_____

What do you want to say to the Father about what He has said?

_____

_____

Take a moment to meditate on the Word(s) that seem more pronounced to you as you read what God has to say. After meditating on what He has said, what do you hear the Holy Spirit speaking to your Heart? Take the Scriptures you found, along with what the Holy Spirit is speaking to your heart, and use them to change and frame your destiny:

_____

_____

_____

Psalm 18

Who can distinguish between his own lapses and mistakes? Father, deliver and declare me innocent from hidden, concealed, and secret sins. Deliver me from unconscious sins; those that have been covered in my own mind, and those I have attempted to defend and conceal from You. Wash me in Your blood. Purge me with spiritual hyssop.

Father, hold me, Your servant, Your worshipper, Your familiar servant, Your beloved, and Your intimate friend. Keep me in check. Let Your Word restrain me from doing or satisfying my own desires. Keep me from the sin of pride, and let me only be filled with Your Word and will. Father, let me not assimilate or be ruled by my own fleshly desires. Let me not form opinions or judgments contrary to Yours.

I submit to the spirit of wisdom and understanding in the knowledge of You. I submit to Your Lordship and declare that no other person, thing, or desire will rule over me. I am complete in You, and my life will have a successful conclusion.

May You find satisfaction and pleasure in what I say. Accept my life and worship. May Your favor, goodwill, and benefits surround me. Cause Your face to shine on me.

Let my expressions be acceptable to You. Let the meditation of my spirit, the thoughts of my mind, the seat of my emotions, my passions, and my appetites be pleasing to You.

You are my rock, my protection, my refuge, and my sword. You are beautiful. You have bought me with Your own blood. I know my Redeemer lives! You have delivered me from all my misfortunes. When blood was required, You shed Yours. Therefore, the power of death, hell, and the grave has no authority over me!

I pray in the authority that is invested in the name of Jesus the Christ. Amen.

Scripture Reference: *Psalm 18*

Prayers to Frame your Prophetic Destiny
Worksheet

(This may be used as a guide to help you begin to frame your destiny.)

My personal Conversation with the Father regarding:

_____

Discover what the Word of God says about:

_____

_____

Search out and write down the verses in the Bible that mention the word(s), phrase(s), or concept(s):

_____

_____

_____

How are these word(s), phrase(s), or concept(s) applicable to you, your family, your church, your community, or your nation?

_____

_____

_____

_____

_____

_____

_____

Prayers to Frame Your Prophetic Destiny

What do you want to say to the Father about what He has said?

_____

_____

_____

Take a moment to meditate on the Word(s) that seem more pronounced to you as you read what God has to say. After meditating on what He has said, what do you hear the Holy Spirit speaking to your Heart? Take the Scriptures you found, along with what the Holy Spirit is speaking to your heart, and use them to change and frame your destiny:

_____

_____

_____

_____

_____

_____

_____

_____

_____

_____

_____

_____

_____

_____

_____

_____

_____

_____

My Daily Bread

Father, I thank You for my daily bread and benefits according to Your Word. Father, I thank You for an abundant life in Christ. I thank You that I am rich through Your blessing. I am rich in Christ, wisdom, revelation knowledge, and understanding. I am rich in love, spiritual gifts, family, and friends.

Father, I acknowledge You, therefore, I am wealthy in every aspect of my life. It is You Who has enabled me and anointed me to make wealth. Confirm Your covenant You swore to my family.

I decree and declare that the blessing on my life extends to every generation. I declare that every generation increases progressively to set up the benefits of the blessing of Abraham perpetually.

I decree and declare according to Your promise:

I am a distinguished nation.

I am blessed with an abundant increase of favors.

My name is famous and extraordinary.

I am a blessing dispensing good to others.

I am a Kingdom producer.

Kings will come from my family.

You will be God to my children.

You will cause me to possess land for an everlasting possession.

Because I am blessed, I will inherit the Earth.

I break and demolish every mindset associated with the spirit of lack. I have a supply in the riches and glory of Christ Jesus. I am debt free. Father, according to Psalm 115 Father, You are mindful of me, You will bless me, and increase me to a greater extent. Therefore, I bind the promise of Abraham to my heart and mind. I bind increase to my life. I bind prosperity to my mind and heart. Establish Your covenant and make me a blessing.

I seal this prayer in the name of Jesus the Christ. Amen.

Scripture references: *John 10:10; Proverbs 10:22; Deuteronomy 8:18; Genesis 12: 1-4; Psalm 37:22*

Conversations of a Watchman

PRAYERS TO FRAME YOUR PROPHETIC DESTINY
WORKSHEET

(This may be used as a guide to help you begin to frame your destiny.)

My personal Conversation with the Father regarding:

_____

Discover what the Word of God says about:

_____
_____

Search out and write down the verses in the Bible that mention the word(s), phrase(s), or concept(s):

_____
_____
_____

How are these word(s), phrase(s), or concept(s) applicable to you, your family, your church, your community, or your nation?

_____
_____
_____
_____
_____
_____
_____
_____

What do you want to say to the Father about what He has said?

_____

_____

_____

Take a moment to meditate on the Word(s) that seem more pronounced to you as you read what God has to say. After meditating on what He has said, what do you hear the Holy Spirit speaking to your Heart? Take the Scriptures you found, along with what the Holy Spirit is speaking to your heart, and use them to change and frame your destiny:

_____
_____
_____
_____
_____
_____
_____
_____
_____
_____
_____
_____
_____
_____
_____
_____
_____

Mending Breaches

Father, I thank You that You long to be gracious to Your people and to show us Your loving kindness. We accept Your victory, Your favor, Your love, Your peace, and Your unbroken companionship. Therefore, be gracious to us and hear our cry. We know if You hear us, You will answer us.

We ask You to forgive us for doing things our own way and making idols of ourselves and others. We repent for worshiping things, positions, success, and people above You. We declare that You are Lord of our lives. Wash us in the blood of Christ, and we shall be clean. Thank You for the redeeming power that exists in the blood of Christ.

Father, we ask that You heal every break, opening, rupture, and split caused by our own disobedience and disregard for Your divine will. Settle and mend every broken relationship caused by alienation, disagreement, discord, disharmony, dissention, division, falling-out, splitting, strife, fracture, and quarreling. We release the love and unity of the Spirit. May the love of God be shed abroad in our hearts by the Holy Spirit; eliminating disaffection, division, divorce, estrangement, indifference, remoteness, separation, setting against, turning away, and withdrawal. May they know us by the love that we show for one another.

Recover or replace everything that we have lost, and make us bridges of Your love and instruments of Your peace. Establish Your agape love among the brethren. Align our hearts and refresh, revive, and rejuvenate Your body in Your love.

Let the Words of this prayer be sealed by the power contained in the name and blood of Jesus the Christ. Amen.

Scripture references*: Ezekiel 22:30; Isaiah 30:19-26; Romans 5:5*

Prayers to Frame your Prophetic Destiny
Worksheet

(This may be used as a guide to help you begin to frame your destiny.)

My personal Conversation with the Father regarding:

_____

Discover what the Word of God says about:

_____
_____
_____

Search out and write down the verses in the Bible that mention the word(s), phrase(s), or concept(s):

_____
_____
_____
_____

How are these word(s), phrase(s), or concept(s) applicable to you, your family, your church, your community, or your nation?

_____
_____
_____
_____
_____
_____
_____
_____

Prayers to Frame Your Prophetic Destiny

What do you want to say to the Father about what He has said?

_____

_____

_____

_____

Take a moment to meditate on the Word(s) that seem more pronounced to you as you read what God has to say. After meditating on what He has said, what do you hear the Holy Spirit speaking to your Heart? Take the Scriptures you found, along with what the Holy Spirit is speaking to your heart, and use them to change and frame your destiny:

_____

_____

_____

_____

_____

_____

_____

_____

_____

_____

_____

_____

_____

_____

_____

_____

_____

_____

_____

Repositioning

Father, the God of Israel, Abraham, Isaac, and Jacob, we agree to revolutionize history by humbling ourselves, praying, seeking Your face, and turning from our wicked ways. Hide not Yourself from us. We willingly yield to Your perfect will.

Father, we acknowledge You have chosen our place before YOU to serve as leaders in the restoration of true apostolic order and Davidic worship. We commit to the reestablishment of all things pertaining to the Kingdom that we may witness the Heavens release the Lord Jesus Christ, Whom the Heavens must retain until the restoration of all things. Father, we declare, restoring Kingdom order is our lives' work.

We declare that we will do it able-bodied, with a sound mind, by Your might, and by Your Spirit. We stand before You presenting ourselves and consecrating ourselves as You have directed!

From the inside out and from the top to the bottom, Father we empty ourselves of our own desires and ask You to establish quickly a firm foundation in our lives!

We seal this prayer in the name of Jesus the Christ. Amen.

Scripture References: *2 Chronicles 7:14-16; 1 Corinthians 14:40; Acts 3:19-21; Acts 15:13-19*

Prayers to Frame Your Prophetic Destiny

Worksheet

(This may be used as a guide to help you begin to frame your destiny.)

My personal Conversation with the Father regarding:

___

Discover what the Word of God says about:

___

Search out and write down the verses in the Bible that mention the word(s), phrase(s), or concept(s):

___

___

How are these word(s), phrase(s), or concept(s) applicable to you, your family, your church, your community, or your nation?

___

___

What do you want to say to the Father about what He has said?

___

___

Take a moment to meditate on the Word(s) that seem more pronounced to you as you read what God has to say. After meditating on what He has said, what do you hear the Holy Spirit speaking to your Heart? Take the Scriptures you found, along with what the Holy Spirit is speaking to your heart, and use them to change and frame your destiny:

___

___

___

A Fresh Confession

"Lord, who was I when I walked with You? Who am I?"

The Lord, Who bought you with the price of His own blood, says: "Though people have looked down on you, and because of your actions have called you worthless, do not be dismayed. For through trials, I have proven, examined and chosen you. I have desired you, preferred you, and loved you."

Father, people will witness, arise, and worship when they notice Your faithfulness upon my life. Because You are a sustainer; the One who carries me through every trial. You are firm and unshakable in all Your ways. You are secure; the One in whom I can confide and trust, the One on whom I can lean and build upon.

I thank You that there is a prophetic call on my life that is associated with divine supernatural power. I thank You that spiritual dominance and heaven-bestowed rulership is conferred upon my life. I thank You in this year I will experience unimpeded growth, unlimited potential, and indomitable opportunity. Others will see and say, "God has appeared and His Kingdom government is ruling." For I acknowledge my priestly calling to minister before You.

I will go wherever You send me. I will walk in the prophetic office to which You have called me. Because of Your divine presence and activity in my life, wealth, prosperity, spiritual well-being, and prophetic operation shall be consistently tangible.

Lord, according to *John 15:3*, I am clean by the Words You have spoken to me. You have purged me that I may bring forth more fruit. Therefore, I remain in constant fellowship with You. Without You, I can do nothing. Father, be gloried in the Son through my life.

Father, cause me to stand firm, and guard Your Words to safely escape the power and assaults of the enemy. I declare, I will not depart from Your Word, but I will acknowledge the Holy Spirit, Who is my helper. I submit to the influence of the Holy Spirit. I will allow His divine influence and energy to continually operate in me. I thank You that I am rooted and grounded in Your love. I have been knitted together with You, by the Holy Spirit. I allow the Holy Spirit to permanently establish Himself within me and exercise His power through me. I declare, my life will remain in a state and condition worthy of Your love. In order to see Your will have preeminence, I die to my fleshly desires and my own will. I remain in fellowship with You waiting for Your Word to manifest!

Father, I surrender my will, mind, heart, body, and soul. Wash me in Your Blood, and cleanse me from unrighteousness. Cause me to echo Your heart and mind. I allow the Holy Spirit free course in my life. I take pleasure in You. I prize You above all else. I desire and long for You, and I am unwilling to abandon or live without You, Your will, Your counsel, Your mind, or Your heart.

Father, take pleasure in me, and prize me above all else. Desire me, and be unwilling to abandon or finish without me. Father, use me. I will remain under Your divine influence by Your wisdom and knowledge so that You and the Father, by the Spirit, may appear and remain in me. Holy Spirit, show me how to continually cultivate my relationship with You, so I can see clearly the heart and mind of the Father displayed through Christ Jesus.

Father, establish Your Kingdom, and bring breakthrough in the spirit realm, so a move of God can have free course between Heaven and Earth.

I declare an open heaven! I maintain the open heaven through my communion with You, the Son, and the Holy Spirit by way of **worship**, **intercession**, and **passionate obedience** to Your voice.

Father, I lay the foundations of the earth with Christ as the Chief cornerstone. I declare that the apostolic and prophetic anointing be released and have free course in my nation, in my country, in my state, in my city, in my region, in my community, and in my family. Establish Your Kingdom in Earth as it is in Heaven.

Father, I prepare the way for the counsel of Your will to be established through prayer. Father, I prepare the way for Your heart and mind to be made manifest in my nation, in my country, in my state, in my city, in my region, in my community, and in my family through prayer. I build by the Spirit for future realities I could not possibly know how to prepare for in the natural.

I seal this prayer in the name of Jesus the Christ. Amen.

Scripture References: Matthew 6:10; John 15:3-7; Ephesians 2:18-22; James 1:17

PRAYERS TO FRAME YOUR PROPHETIC DESTINY
WORKSHEET

(This may be used as a guide to help you begin to frame your destiny.)

My personal Conversation with the Father regarding:

_____

Discover what the Word of God says about:

_____

Search out and write down the verses in the Bible that mention the word(s), phrase(s), or concept(s):

_____

_____

How are these word(s), phrase(s), or concept(s) applicable to you, your family, your church, your community, or your nation?

_____

_____

What do you want to say to the Father about what He has said?

_____

_____

Take a moment to meditate on the Word(s) that seem more pronounced to you as you read what God has to say. After meditating on what He has said, what do you hear the Holy Spirit speaking to your Heart? Take the Scriptures you found, along with what the Holy Spirit is speaking to your heart, and use them to change and frame your destiny:

_____

_____

_____

Committing Your Friendships to God

Father, I declare that the friendships You have given me will help stir a greater passion in me for the love of Christ and the Kingdom of God. As we walk together in Your grace, make us wiser and better. During our Spirit-led conversations, may we become more alert and keen to the promptings of the Holy Spirit, the moving of the Holy Spirit, and the spiritual realm.

As we learn from each other, may the image of Christ become clearer to us and in us. Father, form our character after Your image. Father, let our conversation sharpen each other's wit and promote spiritual revelation in the knowledge of You. May we encourage one another to live out what You have imagined for our lives. I acknowledge You and give back to You what You have given me. I seal my friendships in the blood of Christ, in the name of Jesus the Christ. Amen!

Scriptural Reference: *Hebrews 10:24; Proverbs 27:17*

PRAYERS TO FRAME YOUR PROPHETIC DESTINY
WORKSHEET

(This may be used as a guide to help you begin to frame your destiny.)

My personal Conversation with the Father regarding:

___

Discover what the Word of God says about:

___

Search out and write down the verses in the Bible that mention the word(s), phrase(s), or concept(s):

___

How are these word(s), phrase(s), or concept(s) applicable to you, your family, your church, your community, or your nation?

___

What do you want to say to the Father about what He has said?

___

Take a moment to meditate on the Word(s) that seem more pronounced to you as you read what God has to say. After meditating on what He has said, what do you hear the Holy Spirit speaking to your Heart? Take the Scriptures you found, along with what the Holy Spirit is speaking to your heart, and use them to change and frame your destiny:

___

___

___

God's Provision

Father, I thank You that You cause us to flourish in all things. I thank You that You furnish and generously supply every necessity arising from any circumstance, situation, or case. I thank You that You completely supply every pressing necessity. I thank You that You render perfect every condition marked by deficiency through Your Son, Jesus the Christ.

Scripture Reference: *Philippians 4:19*

PRAYERS TO FRAME YOUR PROPHETIC DESTINY
WORKSHEET

(This may be used as a guide to help you begin to frame your destiny.)

My personal Conversation with the Father regarding:

_____

Discover what the Word of God says about:

_____

Search out and write down the verses in the Bible that mention the word(s), phrase(s), or concept(s):

_____

_____

How are these word(s), phrase(s), or concept(s) applicable to you, your family, your church, your community, or your nation?

_____

_____

What do you want to say to the Father about what He has said?

_____

_____

Take a moment to meditate on the Word(s) that seem more pronounced to you as you read what God has to say. After meditating on what He has said, what do you hear the Holy Spirit speaking to your Heart? Take the Scriptures you found, along with what the Holy Spirit is speaking to your heart, and use them to change and frame your destiny:

_____

_____

_____

Father, Grant Me a Husband

The Lord GRANT you that you may find rest, each of you in the house of her husband.
(Ruth 1:9)

Father, I pray the prayer Naomi prayed for Ruth: "I thank You that You GRANT me that I may find rest in the house of my husband." I trust You that my husband is:

- A man of prayer with prophetic gifting.
- A Worshiper.
- A mighty man of wealth: spiritually, financially, mentally, emotionally, and physically.
- A man of wisdom and understanding.
- A man who has a genuine love for children and the people of God.
- A man who has never been married or is a widow.
- A man who loves me as Christ loves the church.
- A man who manages his money well.
- A man with the Issachar anointing.
- A man who is handsome in my eyes and physically attracts me.
- A man of peace who is not quarrelsome.
- A man willing to leave his father and mother and cleave to me.

- A man of great faith who knows, understands, and applies the Word of God.
- A man who is a tither and a generous giver.
- A man who will stir up and awaken my love.
- A man who owns property and has invested his money wisely.
- A man who knows how to communicate.
- A man who is not selfish.
- A man of vision.
- A man who is a leader.
- A man who walks in kingly dominion and whose head is Christ.
- A man who understands unconditional love.
- A man who is secure and confident in You.
- A man who can interpret prophetic dreams and visions.
- A husband who will trust, praise, and call me blessed.

I seal this prayer in the name of Jesus the Christ. Amen.

Scripture References: *Proverbs 31; Ephesians 5:23; Genesis 1:26*

Prayers to Frame your Prophetic Destiny
Worksheet

(This may be used as a guide to help you begin to frame your destiny.)

My personal Conversation with the Father regarding:

_____

Discover what the Word of God says about:

_____
_____

Search out and write down the verses in the Bible that mention the word(s), phrase(s), or concept(s):

_____
_____
_____

How are these word(s), phrase(s), or concept(s) applicable to you, your family, your church, your community, or your nation?

_____
_____
_____
_____
_____
_____
_____

What do you want to say to the Father about what He has said?

_____
_____
_____

Take a moment to meditate on the Word(s) that seem more pronounced to you as you read what God has to say. After meditating on what He has said, what do you hear the Holy Spirit speaking to your Heart? Take the Scriptures you found, along with what the Holy Spirit is speaking to your heart, and use them to change and frame your destiny:

_____
_____
_____
_____
_____
_____
_____
_____
_____
_____
_____
_____
_____
_____
_____
_____
_____

God's Divine Order

We declare we will exercise DOMINION, rulership, ownership, and control in every area under the mandate You have given us. We declare the sovereign rule of Christ in our lives and over every area to which the Lord gives us authority and influence. We declare land ownership for Kingdom cultivation purposes.

We declare that we are a FRUITFUL people. Therefore, we declare an increase leading to beneficial, profitable, abundant results, and growth for the Kingdom of God in our lives. We declare a grace upon our lives, which comes through Jesus Christ, that is conducive for productivity. We declare that we are abounding in fruit.

We declare the principle of MULTIPLICATION is active in us through the creative Word of God. We declare that we are GREAT people for the Kingdom of God. We declare that we increase and multiply exceedingly and that we are strong Kingdom citizens. We declare that we increase and multiply in our substance in every area, thereby eliminating lack.

We actively REPLENISH every person, place, or thing we come in contact with through the power of the Holy Spirit. We declare that we live life to the full until it overflows because of Christ. We declare that we are accomplished according to the order of God's ORIGINAL INTENTION and DIVINE ORDER. We declare that we are a consecrated people and our hands are full of supply. We are complete and satisfied. We declare that we mutually fill each other's gaps and attack with united strength every empty place. We declare that we bring fresh oil and an authentic supply through the authority of Christ. We declare that we are a people who inspire and nourish others.

Through our passion for Christ, we impose Kingdom mandates wherever we go. We repress and destroy every thought, idea, activity, and action contrary to the counsel of God by the Authority conferred upon us in Christ. We declare we are overcomers in every aspect of our lives. Every place You send us, we declare Your Kingdom come, and Your counsel be established. We expand the Kingdom of God and restrain the kingdom of darkness. We shatter the bands of injustice, disengage intense difficulties, and declare the deliverance of the afflicted. We bring every thought captive to the obedience of Jesus Christ. By the superior force found in the name and blood of Jesus Christ, we overpower every adversary!

We declare that every confused, empty place, every area that lacks a coherent image, formal structure, orderly arrangement, or divine set order, begin to produce and operate according to God's original intention. We declare that every gap, ineffectual, obscure, dark place receive the wind, breath, and mind of God. We declare that the breath of God is moving, and imparting energy, executive and administrative power, and Shekinah glory. We declare that the breath of God is releasing and creating an atmosphere for the creative Word of God to bring about restoration, order, harmony, and wholeness according to God's original purpose.

We declare that every valley be lifted and filled up, and every mountain and hill is made low. We decree and declare that every crooked and uneven place is made straight and level, and the rough places a plain. We declare that the glory of the Lord shall be revealed in our lives, in our families, in our ministry, in the Body of Christ, in our city, in our state, in our country, in our nation, and in our world.

We agree with the Word which declares we are blessed! We are blessed to PROSPER, PRODUCE, FILL THE EARTH, and TAKE OVER wherever we go!

Father, we are looking for You and expecting You to respond. We linger for and eagerly anticipate You to advance on our behalf in order that we may pass through, transform, mature, and spring forth again with KINGLY DOMINION!

We seal this prayer in the name of Jesus the Christ. Amen!

Scripture References: *Genesis 1:2; Hebrews 11:3; Hebrews 1:2-3; Genesis 1:26-28; Genesis 27:40; Hebrews 4:9-10; Isaiah 40: 4-5*

PRAYERS TO FRAME YOUR PROPHETIC DESTINY
WORKSHEET
(This may be used as a guide to help you begin to frame your destiny.)

My personal Conversation with the Father regarding:

_____

Discover what the Word of God says about:

_____

Search out and write down the verses in the Bible that mention the word(s), phrase(s), or concept(s):

_____

_____

How are these word(s), phrase(s), or concept(s) applicable to you, your family, your church, your community, or your nation?

_____

_____

What do you want to say to the Father about what He has said?

_____

_____

Take a moment to meditate on the Word(s) that seem more pronounced to you as you read what God has to say. After meditating on what He has said, what do you hear the Holy Spirit speaking to your Heart? Take the Scriptures you found, along with what the Holy Spirit is speaking to your heart, and use them to change and frame your destiny:

_____

_____

_____

Prayer Quote

"Those persons who know the deep peace of God, the unfathomable peace that passeth all understanding, are always men and women of much prayer."

~ R. A. Torrey

Prayers to Frame Your Prophetic Destiny

The Second Watch

Conversations of a Watchman

Draw Me

Your love is better than wine,
Your name is like perfume poured out,
Draw me and I will run after You;
You whom my soul loves.

I am humbled by Your love,
Your love waves like a banner over me,
It protects and comforts me,
You are beautiful — my delight.

I will rejoice in You when I remember Your love,
For You cause me to grow in deep and difficult places.
Altogether lovely,
Chief among ten thousand to my soul.

I am my Beloved's,
His desire is toward me.
He sings,
Come away my love,
Your winter has past.

Scripture Reference: *Song of Solomon 1*

Prayers to Frame your Prophetic Destiny
Worksheet

(This may be used as a guide to help you begin to frame your destiny.)

My personal Conversation with the Father regarding:

___

Discover what the Word of God says about:

___

Search out and write down the verses in the Bible that mention the word(s), phrase(s), or concept(s):

___

___

How are these word(s), phrase(s), or concept(s) applicable to you, your family, your church, your community, or your nation?

___

___

What do you want to say to the Father about what He has said?

___

___

Take a moment to meditate on the Word(s) that seem more pronounced to you as you read what God has to say. After meditating on what He has said, what do you hear the Holy Spirit speaking to your Heart? Take the Scriptures you found, along with what the Holy Spirit is speaking to your heart, and use them to change and frame your destiny:

___

___

___

A Song of Solomon

I am intoxicated by You,
Mentally and emotionally intoxicated by Your love.
I am infatuated, and inspired by You,
Enthralled, captivated, and absorbed by You.

Your name alone attracts me,
How precious is the name of Jesus,
You are the oil,
Your name is the oil poured on us.

For Your name's sake;
Pour Your glory on us,
Pour Yourself on us,
Empty the essence of who You are,
Spreading the fragrance of Your name on us.

Through Your name I am preserved,
Spread the fragrance of Your name;
You, whom my soul loves,
I am soothed by the wonder of Your name.
I am drawn by Your beauty and glory alone.
In the secret place of Your chambers, I find intimate fellowship;
Coming to know and be known,

Seeing and being seen,
Hearing and being heard.

In the secret place, my future unfolds,
My life is revealed in the center of Your firm hold.
I am completely made whole in Your love,
My beauty is a reflection of Your accepting love.
You are my intimate friend and lover,
My heart palpitates at the thought of You,
At the thought of Your desire toward me,
My breath is taken away.

Scripture Reference: *Song of Solomon*

Prayers to Frame your Prophetic Destiny
Worksheet
(This may be used as a guide to help you begin to frame your destiny.)

My personal Conversation with the Father regarding:

_____

Discover what the Word of God says about:

_____
_____
_____

Search out and write down the verses in the Bible that mention the word(s), phrase(s), or concept(s):

_____
_____
_____
_____

How are these word(s), phrase(s), or concept(s) applicable to you, your family, your church, your community, or your nation?

_____
_____
_____
_____
_____
_____
_____
_____

What do you want to say to the Father about what He has said?

_____

_____

_____

Take a moment to meditate on the Word(s) that seem more pronounced to you as you read what God has to say. After meditating on what He has said, what do you hear the Holy Spirit speaking to your Heart? Take the Scriptures you found, along with what the Holy Spirit is speaking to your heart, and use them to change and frame your destiny:

_____
_____
_____
_____
_____
_____
_____
_____
_____
_____
_____
_____
_____
_____
_____
_____
_____

Your Character

You are Guiltless and Sinless

Your strength, power, and might is imparted to and discovered by those who love You.

You were despised, held in contempt, considered worthless, considered unworthy of notice, and made destitute. You became frail. You were refused love and unaccepted by men. You experienced mental and physical pain, inexpressible grief; a torturing of Your soul, deep disappointment, loss, and guilt. You knew internal and external sickness, affliction, sadness, disease, and grief. You were not valued.

Certainly, You have forgiven, carried, and laid upon Yourself, our diseases, sicknesses, sadness, weaknesses, and distresses. You were punished so my desire may be upon You and my longing toward You. You have accepted me. You received the penalty I deserved.

You were treated as common and defiled for my faults and rebellion. You were broken in pieces, oppressed, broken in spirit, and made inferior for my failure and guilt. You tolerated correction, discipline, and instruction. By Your wounds, I am restored to favor, healed of distresses, and hurts. Because of You, I am mended and comforted.

You became completely separated from God, and became an offense that I might be **acceptable to God.**

You were without blame, faultless, free from condemnation or judgment, but You became an offense that I might be **acceptable to God**.

You are Altogether Lovely

O taste and see that the Lord is good. The kiss of the Lord is a sweet thing. You are the object of my desire. You are that which my eyes desire — my delight, Who is full of grace and beauty. You are the precious lover of my soul.

You are Good

Father, Your nature is pleasant, excellent, distinguished, upright, and honorable. You are the Tree of Life. You are inclined to goodness. You are the Gift of gifts. May Your **Goodness** flow through me and may I be free from any desire to manipulate people. I submit my thoughts to You that my communication may please and praise You. You are Kind, and You are Generous.

You are Faithful

Father, You are stable. You are **steadfast,** tenacious, unfaltering, unswerving, persistent, untiring, relentless, dedicated, devoted, loyal, enthusiastic, fanatical, **passionate**, loving, obsessive, committed, sturdy, powerful, and firm. You are a **secure** shelter. Your Word is **True**. You are unwavering, **constant**, steady, and fixed. You fulfill Your promises. Your faithfulness is Your strength.

You are Trustworthy

You are worthy of trust. You are faithful in every transaction. You are reliable, One Who can be relied on, and One in Whom I can confide. You remain while others change.

You are Full of Humility

As Christ submitted Himself by a lowly spirit to the will and power of God, I submit myself by a lowly spirit to the will and power of God. I bring down all pride, and make myself low before You. I acknowledge that I cannot do anything on my own. I need Your ability and Your power.

You are True

You are perfectly true, the very essence of God, an absolute force, and the perfect expression of truth. In You, Christ, we see God as He is, without partiality. You fulfill the meaning of Your name. You are true to Your Word and Sound. You cannot lie. You are marked by truth. Therefore, I allow truth to reign in me that I may be free from dishonesty, deceit, pretense, and falsehood.

You are Just

You maintain what is right. You are righteous. You reward, and You punish. Your words are fulfilled because You are righteous. You love truth and wisdom. You are righteous in government, righteous in Your cause, righteous in conduct, and character. You are justified and vindicated by God. You are perfect in all of Your ways.

You judge according to divine standards because there is perfect agreement between Your nature and Your actions. You are authentic. You act in complete conformity to the will of God because You are holy. You are **acceptable to God.**

Father, I acknowledge your sovereignty. You are righteous in ALL of Your ways. Cause me to love truth and wisdom. Because of You, I am **accepted in the beloved.**

We seal this prayer in the name of Jesus the Christ. Amen.

Scripture References: *Song of Solomon 5:16; Matthew 19:16; Isaiah 11; 1 Thessalonians 5:24; Philippians 2:4; John 1:14; Zechariah 9:9; John 5:30; Acts 22:14; Isaiah 53; 1 Peter 1:18-19; Ephesians 1:6*

Prayers to Frame your Prophetic Destiny
Worksheet
(This may be used as a guide to help you begin to frame your destiny.)

My personal Conversation with the Father regarding:

_____

Discover what the Word of God says about:

_____
_____
_____

Search out and write down the verses in the Bible that mention the word(s), phrase(s), or concept(s):

_____
_____
_____
_____

How are these word(s), phrase(s), or concept(s) applicable to you, your family, your church, your community, or your nation?

_____
_____
_____
_____
_____
_____
_____
_____

What do you want to say to the Father about what He has said?

Take a moment to meditate on the Word(s) that seem more pronounced to you as you read what God has to say. After meditating on what He has said, what do you hear the Holy Spirit speaking to your Heart? Take the Scriptures you found, along with what the Holy Spirit is speaking to your heart, and use them to change and frame your destiny:

Eat Your Portion

There is a predetermined path for you;

walk in it.

There is a banquet table prepared for you.

Eat what is prepared for you.

Eat only your portion and not the portion of another.

You can only process what has been prepared for you.

When you eat another's portion,

You will only vomit because it is not yours to digest.

Your system will only absorb what is prepared for you.

Eat what has been prepared for you.

In your portion, You will find strength and complete

satisfaction.

I AM your Portion.

Scriptural References: *Romans 8:21-30; Song of Solomon 2:4; Psalm 73:26; Psalm 119:57; Psalm 142:5; Lamentations 3:24*

PRAYERS TO FRAME YOUR PROPHETIC DESTINY
WORKSHEET

(This may be used as a guide to help you begin to frame your destiny.)

My personal Conversation with the Father regarding:

_____

Discover what the Word of God says about:

_____

Search out and write down the verses in the Bible that mention the word(s), phrase(s), or concept(s):

_____

_____

How are these word(s), phrase(s), or concept(s) applicable to you, your family, your church, your community, or your nation?

_____

_____

What do you want to say to the Father about what He has said?

_____

_____

Take a moment to meditate on the Word(s) that seem more pronounced to you as you read what God has to say. After meditating on what He has said, what do you hear the Holy Spirit speaking to your Heart? Take the Scriptures you found, along with what the Holy Spirit is speaking to your heart, and use them to change and frame your destiny:

_____

_____

_____

A Place by Me

Let down your guard, and come lay prostrate before Me. Refresh yourself, and drink from My Springs to quench your thirst. In laying down, you shall discover the keys for abundant life and the power to subdue your territory. I will pour water on your wounds, and you will recover.

I am your Creator. Here in the place of surrender, the place by Me, I will form and frame you for your destiny. *(The word "formed" is the same word used in Genesis when it says that I formed man out of the dust of the ground, the same word when I spoke to Jeremiah about being formed in his mother's womb, and the same word when I spoke of making summer and winter. It is the same word used when I spoke of forming the dry land.)* I have already predestined, predetermined, and devised a plan for your life that you may serve Me, and serve a people. By My covenant, I have established it.

Bring yourself into a place of consecration. Come and dwell and build your habitation in Me. As you abide in Me, you will know, and understand that I AM everything. AM I not a Father Who provides for His children? Therefore, listen, hear with pleasure, pay attention, and be of an understanding heart.

I AM He who hears and answers when you cry. I AM attentive to your call. Cry out! Sing! Declare and decree! I am watching over My Word to perform it. Call from the North! Call from the South! Call from the East! Call from the West! Gather what you need from the four corners of the Earth. For in My house there is complete provision.

My Words are not those of a man. Listen, hear with pleasure, pay attention, and be of an understanding heart. The Words that I speak they are Spirit, and they are Life. Heed My counsel, and go forward!

Scriptural References*: Genesis 2:7; Isaiah 44:3; Jeremiah 1:5; Psalm 36: 7-9*

Conversations of a Watchman

PRAYERS TO FRAME YOUR PROPHETIC DESTINY
WORKSHEET

(This may be used as a guide to help you begin to frame your destiny.)

My personal Conversation with the Father regarding:

_____

Discover what the Word of God says about:

_____
_____
_____

Search out and write down the verses in the Bible that mention the word(s), phrase(s), or concept(s):

_____
_____
_____
_____

How are these word(s), phrase(s), or concept(s) applicable to you, your family, your church, your community, or your nation?

_____
_____
_____
_____
_____
_____
_____
_____

Prayers to Frame Your Prophetic Destiny

What do you want to say to the Father about what He has said?

_____
_____
_____

Take a moment to meditate on the Word(s) that seem more pronounced to you as you read what God has to say. After meditating on what He has said, what do you hear the Holy Spirit speaking to your Heart? Take the Scriptures you found, along with what the Holy Spirit is speaking to your heart, and use them to change and frame your destiny:

_____
_____
_____
_____
_____
_____
_____
_____
_____
_____
_____
_____
_____
_____
_____
_____
_____

Arise and Shine

Arise and shine for the Lord has come, and the Glory of the Lord has risen upon you. Arise! Go Forward! Arise! Go Forward!

Arise in your thinking! Go forward in your actions! In your going forward, I will send help from My sanctuary. This is your day, and this is your time. I have given you a future and a hope. Mature in your confidence toward Me. I am giving you a portion that you may increase and flourish.

Stand up in a hostile sense. Openly oppose and resist. Take an offensive position against your enemy. Walk in My power. Cause My Word to come on the scene. Through the Word, preserve yourself from failure and rejection. Maintain your position in the face of attack. Continue in and sustain a life of victory.

Agree with My Word that you may be firm and stable. Then, you will increase, multiply, bring into existence My promises, and your position will be made favorable. Have I not spoken, and will I not bring it to pass? Your agreement with My Word will bring about an outward sign. You will be empowered to bring about results and a distinctive impression, so My very essence is revealed and persists.

Scripture References: *Isaiah 60*

Prayers to Frame your Prophetic Destiny
Worksheet

(This may be used as a guide to help you begin to frame your destiny.)

My personal Conversation with the Father regarding:

_____

Discover what the Word of God says about:

_____

Search out and write down the verses in the Bible that mention the word(s), phrase(s), or concept(s):

_____

_____

How are these word(s), phrase(s), or concept(s) applicable to you, your family, your church, your community, or your nation?

_____

_____

What do you want to say to the Father about what He has said?

_____

_____

Take a moment to meditate on the Word(s) that seem more pronounced to you as you read what God has to say. After meditating on what He has said, what do you hear the Holy Spirit speaking to your Heart? Take the Scriptures you found, along with what the Holy Spirit is speaking to your heart, and use them to change and frame your destiny:

_____

_____

_____

Be Restored

When you make the decision to come and drink from My fountain and lay prostrate before Me, you will see My original intent and divine activity. In the place by Me, you will conceive what is predetermined, and inevitable. Come and see what I have purposed. I will accomplish what I set out to perform. As you surrender to Me, you will produce fruit that will remain. Allow Me to prepare you. I am attending to you and putting your life in order because you are Mine.

As you lay before Me, you will give birth to every purpose and plan. I will bring forth! I will deliver! It is I that impregnates! It is I that causes growth! It is I that brings forth and delivers! Surrender to the process that I may bring about what I have ordained.

In this time, I will rebuild what was destroyed. I will heal every injury and make you whole again. Everything that was stripped and spoiled, I will restore. From the remains you will rise. I will give you beauty for ashes. Out of the heap will rise one that I have formed and fashioned for My purpose. It is I that heals you. If I heal a thing, is it not healed? If I restore a thing, is it not restored? BE HEALED! BE RESTORED!

Scriptural References: *Psalm 51:12; Isaiah 61:3; Jeremiah 30:17; Joel 2:26*

PRAYERS TO FRAME YOUR PROPHETIC DESTINY
WORKSHEET

(This may be used as a guide to help you begin to frame your destiny.)

My personal Conversation with the Father regarding:

_____

Discover what the Word of God says about:

_____

Search out and write down the verses in the Bible that mention the word(s), phrase(s), or concept(s):

_____

_____

How are these word(s), phrase(s), or concept(s) applicable to you, your family, your church, your community, or your nation?

_____

_____

What do you want to say to the Father about what He has said?

_____

_____

Take a moment to meditate on the Word(s) that seem more pronounced to you as you read what God has to say. After meditating on what He has said, what do you hear the Holy Spirit speaking to your Heart? Take the Scriptures you found, along with what the Holy Spirit is speaking to your heart, and use them to change and frame your destiny:

_____

_____

_____

The Breeze of My Spirit

I will cause the breeze and wind of My Spirit to blow on you. The wind of the Lord blows. Do you not perceive the direction in which it blows? In this wind, My mind, counsel, and thoughts will flow and pour into the vessel found longing; the vessel found pursuing. In your pursuit, you will be found of Me. The wind of the Lord will overtake you as you run with pre-ordained grace on your life.

Scriptural References: Psalm 42; Isaiah 41:17-20; Matthew 5:6; John 3:8; John 14:13-15; John 6:35

PRAYERS TO FRAME YOUR PROPHETIC DESTINY
WORKSHEET

(This may be used as a guide to help you begin to frame your destiny.)

My personal Conversation with the Father regarding:

Discover what the Word of God says about:

Search out and write down the verses in the Bible that mention the word(s), phrase(s), or concept(s):

How are these word(s), phrase(s), or concept(s) applicable to you, your family, your church, your community, or your nation?

What do you want to say to the Father about what He has said?

Take a moment to meditate on the Word(s) that seem more pronounced to you as you read what God has to say. After meditating on what He has said, what do you hear the Holy Spirit speaking to your Heart? Take the Scriptures you found, along with what the Holy Spirit is speaking to your heart, and use them to change and frame your destiny:

A Time of Refreshing

Hurry, and plant your seed,

The times of refreshing are upon you.

There is a fresh rain on the horizon,

Hurry, and plant your seed,

Whatever is sown will spring forth in abundance.

Scriptural References: *Joel 2:23-27*

Prayers to Frame Your Prophetic Destiny
Worksheet

(This may be used as a guide to help you begin to frame your destiny.)

My personal Conversation with the Father regarding:

_____

Discover what the Word of God says about:

_____

Search out and write down the verses in the Bible that mention the word(s), phrase(s), or concept(s):

_____

_____

How are these word(s), phrase(s), or concept(s) applicable to you, your family, your church, your community, or your nation?

_____

_____

What do you want to say to the Father about what He has said?

_____

_____

Take a moment to meditate on the Word(s) that seem more pronounced to you as you read what God has to say. After meditating on what He has said, what do you hear the Holy Spirit speaking to your Heart? Take the Scriptures you found, along with what the Holy Spirit is speaking to your heart, and use them to change and frame your destiny:

_____

_____

_____

Generational Blessings

There is a generational blessing of My Word, healing, good will; and the visitation of My Spirit to every subsequent generation.

What I speak to you, I speak to the generations after you,

My Word extends from generation to generation.

I have visited you to restore you.

Though you have been in darkness,

I have come to enlighten you.

I call you to life again,

Lift up your countenance,

Be refreshed,

Be glad.

I have come to make your face shine, to give you wisdom, and kindle your fire. I have come that you may see clearly the promise is from generation to generation.

Scriptural References: *Deuteronomy 7:9; 1 Chronicles 16:15; Psalm 105:8; Luke 1:50*

PRAYERS TO FRAME YOUR PROPHETIC DESTINY

WORKSHEET

(This may be used as a guide to help you begin to frame your destiny.)

My personal Conversation with the Father regarding:

_____

Discover what the Word of God says about:

_____

Search out and write down the verses in the Bible that mention the word(s), phrase(s), or concept(s):

_____

_____

How are these word(s), phrase(s), or concept(s) applicable to you, your family, your church, your community, or your nation?

_____

_____

What do you want to say to the Father about what He has said?

_____

_____

Take a moment to meditate on the Word(s) that seem more pronounced to you as you read what God has to say. After meditating on what He has said, what do you hear the Holy Spirit speaking to your Heart? Take the Scriptures you found, along with what the Holy Spirit is speaking to your heart, and use them to change and frame your destiny:

_____

_____

_____

The Day of Release

THIS IS THE DAY OF RELEASE. In My covenant there is provision for your release. My eyes have been on you, so shall the light of My Word shine out of your darkness. I have numbered and established your days. You will live before Me all the days of your life because I have placed a shield around you.

Today I extend My promise of release through the blood of the everlasting covenant. It is a covenant of peace, and whoever will come under this covenant will enjoy tranquility. I placed you in a position to surround you and guard you. I am your protector, defender, and your military force.

Have I not said, "Those who seek will find, and those who knock, the door will be open?" I have placed an open door before you that you may walk before Me in peace and victory.

Scripture References: *Numbers 25:12; Isaiah 54; Ezekiel 34:11-31; Hebrews 13:20-21*

PRAYERS TO FRAME YOUR PROPHETIC DESTINY
WORKSHEET

(This may be used as a guide to help you begin to frame your destiny.)

My personal Conversation with the Father regarding:

Discover what the Word of God says about:

Search out and write down the verses in the Bible that mention the word(s), phrase(s), or concept(s):

How are these word(s), phrase(s), or concept(s) applicable to you, your family, your church, your community, or your nation?

What do you want to say to the Father about what He has said?

Take a moment to meditate on the Word(s) that seem more pronounced to you as you read what God has to say. After meditating on what He has said, what do you hear the Holy Spirit speaking to your Heart? Take the Scriptures you found, along with what the Holy Spirit is speaking to your heart, and use them to change and frame your destiny:

Conversations of a Watchman

The Hand of the Lord

The Hand of the Lord is on the righteous,
They will not be moved.
The Hand of the Lord is for the righteous,
They will not be overwhelmed.
The Hand of the Lord goes before the righteous,
They shall not be dumbfounded.

This is the season that you will see the Hand of the Lord.
Because you have sought My face and not My hand,
My Hand will go before you,
My Hand will be with you,
My Hand will be upon you, and work for you.

The Hand of the Lord will split the boulders in your path.
The Hand of the Lord will pave the road before you,
The Hand of the Lord will make your path smooth.
The Hand of the Lord will remove every obstacle,
The Hand of the Lord will make your way clear.
The Hand of the Lord will be on you, and you will recover.
The Hand of the Lord will cause you to rise above.

As My Hand goes before you,
Run swiftly in the way I have chosen for you.
Run with a new strength, power, and wisdom.

Prayers to Frame Your Prophetic Destiny

My Hand has gone before you,
My Hand will empower you to finish the work.

Rely on My Hand, and you will do great exploits.
Look for My Hand, and you will know the way to go.
Your times are in My Hand.

Scripture References: *Exodus 7:4-5; Psalm 31:15; 2 Samuel 24:14; 1 King 18:46; 2 Kings 3:15; Ezekiel 33:22; Ezra 7:6-26; Isaiah 62:3; Ezekiel 1:3; Ezekiel 8:1; Ezekiel 3:22; Ezekiel 40:1*

Prayers to Frame your Prophetic Destiny
Worksheet

(This may be used as a guide to help you begin to frame your destiny.)

My personal Conversation with the Father regarding:

_____

Discover what the Word of God says about:

_____
_____
_____

Search out and write down the verses in the Bible that mention the word(s), phrase(s), or concept(s):

_____
_____
_____
_____

How are these word(s), phrase(s), or concept(s) applicable to you, your family, your church, your community, or your nation?

_____
_____
_____
_____
_____
_____
_____
_____

Prayers to Frame Your Prophetic Destiny

What do you want to say to the Father about what He has said?

_____
_____
_____

Take a moment to meditate on the Word(s) that seem more pronounced to you as you read what God has to say. After meditating on what He has said, what do you hear the Holy Spirit speaking to your Heart? Take the Scriptures you found, along with what the Holy Spirit is speaking to your heart, and use them to change and frame your destiny:

_____
_____
_____
_____
_____
_____
_____
_____
_____
_____
_____
_____
_____
_____
_____
_____
_____

An Open Gate

There is an open gate for you. Walk in it and experience the newness of the Spirit flowing. This is a new season.

Go forward. Possess and take over every barren place. I have given you the power and the ability. My covenant shall stand sure. Wait not. Do not delay. My timing and season is now. Go forward. Move forward. Your time has not passed. I have breathed on you to bring renewal, recompense, and restoration.

Just as I breathed into Adam and he became a living soul, I have breathed into you. My life is in you. Therefore, you have been activated for abundant living. Walk in the life provided for you. My hand is upon you, and I will accomplish My pleasure in you.

Come, come, I will cause you to ride on the wings of My Spirit. Ascend with your worship. There you will see Me, and know Me. I will reveal and unveil Myself there in the place of worship. I desire pure, true worship. Worship Me. Worship Me.

Plow not in foreign lands, for I will give you the lands to plow. Plow where I have placed you. Plow where I lead you. Where I lead, there will be an unveiling and a revealing of Myself.

Scripture Reference: Exodus 14:15

Prayers to Frame Your Prophetic Destiny

Worksheet

(This may be used as a guide to help you begin to frame your destiny.)

My personal Conversation with the Father regarding:

___

Discover what the Word of God says about:

___

Search out and write down the verses in the Bible that mention the word(s), phrase(s), or concept(s):

___

How are these word(s), phrase(s), or concept(s) applicable to you, your family, your church, your community, or your nation?

___

What do you want to say to the Father about what He has said?

___

Take a moment to meditate on the Word(s) that seem more pronounced to you as you read what God has to say. After meditating on what He has said, what do you hear the Holy Spirit speaking to your Heart? Take the Scriptures you found, along with what the Holy Spirit is speaking to your heart, and use them to change and frame your destiny:

___
___
___

Hear, Listen, and Obey

Hear, listen, and obey. I will give you the ability to hear and agree with what I have promised. In your yielding, your request is granted. Hear with an accepting heart what I have promised. Hear My plans and purposes, rumors, and reports.

Prayers to Frame Your Prophetic Destiny

I will Hear, Listen, and Obey

Father, I choose to remain in a place to know Your original design; the place where divine purpose, and plans are formed, released, pre-ordained, and pre-determined. I will dwell in the secret place under the shadow of Your wings. You are my fortress, my dwelling place, my habitation, my secret hiding place. As I remain in You, cause me to know Your innermost part–Your heart. You are my abundant compensation.

I am ready to obey. Frame my life, and accomplish Your will and purpose in me. Speak to me, so I can produce fruits of righteousness. Prepare me and make my life an offering. Attend to me and order my steps in Your Word. Bring to pass what You have ordained. I belong to You!

I offer myself as a living sacrifice. Press my life, so Your oil may flow freely through me. Creator, fashion my life. You have deposited in me the ability to increase and be successful. I abide in You as You complete me.

I seal this prayer in the name of Jesus the Christ. Amen.

Scriptural References: *Deuteronomy 30:20; Psalm 91; Romans 12:1; Romans 8:21-31; 2 Corinthians 9:10*

Prayers to Frame your Prophetic Destiny
Worksheet

(This may be used as a guide to help you begin to frame your destiny.)

My personal Conversation with the Father regarding:

_____

Discover what the Word of God says about:

_____

_____

Search out and write down the verses in the Bible that mention the word(s), phrase(s), or concept(s):

_____

_____

_____

How are these word(s), phrase(s), or concept(s) applicable to you, your family, your church, your community, or your nation?

_____

_____

_____

_____

_____

_____

_____

Prayers to Frame Your Prophetic Destiny

What do you want to say to the Father about what He has said?

_____
_____
_____

Take a moment to meditate on the Word(s) that seem more pronounced to you as you read what God has to say. After meditating on what He has said, what do you hear the Holy Spirit speaking to your Heart? Take the Scriptures you found, along with what the Holy Spirit is speaking to your heart, and use them to change and frame your destiny:

_____
_____
_____
_____
_____
_____
_____
_____
_____
_____
_____
_____
_____
_____
_____
_____
_____

The Promise of a River

My desire is toward you. Can you discern the breath of My eager pursuit of you? My love for you is perpetual and unending. With My constant goodness, kindness, faithfulness, and abiding favor, I have seized you as My own, to establish, recreate, and cause you to continue. In this season, you will advance and quicken your pace.

You will plant spiritual vineyards where people may drink of the new wine of My Spirit. I am raising up true watchmen that will bring My people to a place where they may commune with Me. There is a people who have stayed relentlessly on their ward to see and watch for Me. This is My remnant.

I will bring them, draw them, and gather them together as a shepherd gathers his sheep to nourish and protect. They will come. From this people will flow a stream, a river that flows from My throne into the Earth.

This people, My people, will walk before Me with clean hands and pure hearts because of their intimacy with Me, because of My covenant, and because of My Name by which I have called them.

Then a new song will arise in Zion that will cause the radiance of My Son to shine and the river of My Spirit to flow. The Light of My Son will warm the coldest of hearts, and the river will water the faint and thirsty souls of My beloved. This people will I abundantly satisfy with Myself. I have heard the cries of repentance and have seen the longing heart and My desire is toward them.

PRAYERS TO FRAME YOUR PROPHETIC DESTINY
WORKSHEET

(This may be used as a guide to help you begin to frame your destiny.)

My personal Conversation with the Father regarding:

_____

Discover what the Word of God says about:

_____

Search out and write down the verses in the Bible that mention the word(s), phrase(s), or concept(s):

_____

_____

How are these word(s), phrase(s), or concept(s) applicable to you, your family, your church, your community, or your nation?

_____

What do you want to say to the Father about what He has said?

_____

_____

Take a moment to meditate on the Word(s) that seem more pronounced to you as you read what God has to say. After meditating on what He has said, what do you hear the Holy Spirit speaking to your Heart? Take the Scriptures you found, along with what the Holy Spirit is speaking to your heart, and use them to change and frame your destiny:

_____

_____

_____

Timing and Destiny

You pant for Me as the deer pants for water. You long for Me. Do you not know that I pant and long for you too?

You thought you needed a specific platform to accomplish what I have placed in your heart, but I have given you a new platform from which you will fulfill what I have promised, *Timing and Destiny.*

Be not confused or bitter. It is My hand that has done this to bring you to a place beside Me. Only yield to the season upon you. This season is a time of remolding, a time of remaking. As the clay is in the potter's hand, so you are in My hand and I will make you another vessel. Only yield to the process. Yield to the season. Yield to the timing. For in your yielding, you will find your timing and destiny in Me.

PRAYERS TO FRAME YOUR PROPHETIC DESTINY
WORKSHEET

(This may be used as a guide to help you begin to frame your destiny.)

My personal Conversation with the Father regarding:

_____

Discover what the Word of God says about:

_____

Search out and write down the verses in the Bible that mention the word(s), phrase(s), or concept(s):

_____

_____

How are these word(s), phrase(s), or concept(s) applicable to you, your family, your church, your community, or your nation?

_____

_____

What do you want to say to the Father about what He has said?

_____

_____

Take a moment to meditate on the Word(s) that seem more pronounced to you as you read what God has to say. After meditating on what He has said, what do you hear the Holy Spirit speaking to your Heart? Take the Scriptures you found, along with what the Holy Spirit is speaking to your heart, and use them to change and frame your destiny:

_____

_____

_____

Prayer Quote

"God does nothing except in answer to Prayer."

~ John Wesley

Prayers to Frame Your Prophetic Destiny

The Third Watch

A Word to California

California would not be in your heart if it were not in My heart. For not only is California in My heart, but also My eye is on California. I will come upon that great state like a wave, in the south first, then in the north. My Spirit will move from both ends of the state toward the middle. Though the enemy has set up a wicked platform, I will raise a righteous platform in California; a spiritual wave it will be called.

A Prayer for California

We stand in the gap and repent on behalf of California. Forgive us for our idolatrous ways. Forgive us for the perversion that comes up before You from our state. Father, forgive us for possessing hearts filled with selfish-ambition, greed, and murder. Cleanse us from defilement that has come through the spirit of death, the spirit of Molech, the love of Mammon, and the worship of idols.

Let the blood of Christ appease Your anger and advert the judgment You have determined for the State of California. We apply the Blood of Christ over the entire state of California. Father, remember Your covenantal roots that You have established in this great state.

We uproot, pull down, tear down, and destroy every evil root structure in the name of Jesus the Christ. In its place we build and plant in righteousness in the state of California through continual acts of righteousness. We declare that the Earth of California is the Lord's and the fullness thereof, the world, and they that dwell in California. We declare this is the generation of them who seek You and seek Your face.

As the believers in California intercede from our place in Christ Jesus, who is head of all things, we declare the principalities and powers over this state will NOT be able to subdue the headship of the Lord Jesus Christ, *Who is the Head of all principality and power (Colossians 2:10).*

Awaken and ignite an unquenchable flame of Your Spirit in the hearts and minds of those in this generation that would blaze down to a thousand generations.

Father, we ask You to use us to unite the believers in this area, and allow us to birth forth an awakening that leads to worldwide revival.

In the Name of Jesus the Christ. Amen.

Scripture Reference: *Ps. 24:16*

PRAYERS TO FRAME YOUR PROPHETIC DESTINY
WORKSHEET

(This may be used as a guide to help you begin to frame your destiny.)

My personal Conversation with the Father regarding:

_____

Discover what the Word of God says about:

_____

Search out and write down the verses in the Bible that mention the word(s), phrase(s), or concept(s):

_____

_____

How are these word(s), phrase(s), or concept(s) applicable to you, your family, your church, your community, or your nation?

_____

_____

What do you want to say to the Father about what He has said?

_____

_____

Take a moment to meditate on the Word(s) that seem more pronounced to you as you read what God has to say. After meditating on what He has said, what do you hear the Holy Spirit speaking to your Heart? Take the Scriptures you found, along with what the Holy Spirit is speaking to your heart, and use them to change and frame your destiny:

_____

_____

_____

Breakthrough Prayer

And Asa cried unto the LORD his God, and said, LORD, [it is] nothing with thee to help, whether with many, or with them that have no power: help us, O LORD our God; for we rest on thee, and in thy name we go against this multitude. O LORD, thou [art] our God; let not man prevail against thee (2 Chronicles 14:11).

Father, we cry out like King Asa, "Lord it is nothing with You to help the one with power or the one without power. Help us O Lord our God, for we rest on You and in Your name as we go against this multitude."

Father, You are El Elyon, the Most High God. Let not man, principality, powers, rulers of darkness, wickedness in neither high places, nor demonic strongholds prevail against our family's destiny and pre-ordained purpose. Father, You are the God of Abraham, Isaac, and Jacob. You are Our God Who fulfills Your covenant promises.

Father, purify us with spiritual myrrh that we may be a sweet-smelling fragrance in Your nostrils. Anoint us and cleanse us from selfish ambition, bitterness, feelings of rejection, and abandonment. We bow down and humble ourselves before You.

Give us the anointing of Esther to prophetically shift nations, governments, regions, cities, communities, neighborhoods, businesses, churches, families, friends, education, and individuals.

Give us the anointing of Mordecai that we may stand against and expose the spirit of Haman that would seek to destroy the wells of righteousness and gain control of our nations, government, region, cities, communities, neighborhoods, businesses, churches, families, friends, and schools.

Give us a pure heart, show us favor, and hear us that we may destroy every Amalekite spirit that seeks to delay and deter our destiny. Father, strengthen every weak area in our lives. Where we are weak, Your strength shows up perfectly.

Father, guard our gates by the covenant blood of Jesus Christ. In our intimate times with You, reveal the strategies of the enemy. Reveal the strategies that will defeat the enemy in our nations, government, region, cities, communities, neighborhoods, businesses, churches, families, friends, schools, us, and in the individuals with whom we have influence.

Father, we are willing to sacrifice reputation, position, and acceptance to see Your will be accomplished and Your people walking in liberty. God, do a saving work through us.

Father, we give way to Your direction. May the prophetic wind of Your Holy Spirit give us revelation that will empower us to overcome the warfare at the spiritual gates.

We know that the Holy Spirit distributes the gifts as He wills, but we ask for the spirit of discernment to be cultivated in us and to operate freely in our lives and ministry. Father, we submit and yield to You the prophetic intercessory gift and every spiritual gift You have given us to accomplish Your will. Let the gifts flow purely and unhindered. We submit to those You have placed over us. Father, give us a teachable and accountable spirit. We cast down judgmental and critical spirits in ourselves. We resist spirits of witchcraft, control, and manipulation. We submit to the leading and direction of Your Spirit.

We refuse evil reports against our pastor, our leadership, and the Body of Christ. We give no place to negativity, doubt, and unbelief. We cast out the spirit of bitterness. We forgive those who have rejected, disappointed, or wounded us.

We cast out every unclean, religious, seducing, bitter, demonic spirit that has gained entrance into our lives and ministry. We shut the gates and apply the blood of Jesus Christ as a seal over the doors of our lives, and release a pure prophetic anointing on our lives and our ministry.

Father, we repent for opening the door to the spirits of Jezebel, fear, doubt, and unbelief in our own lives. We demolish every demonic stronghold and command them to go. Anoint us and set our faces like a flint to smite the enemy and to destroy all of the schemes and devices of the enemy. We come against all false prophesy, false prophets, false worship, and false teachings. We tear down every imagination and high thing that would exalt itself against the knowledge of God. We bring every thought captive to the obedience of Jesus Christ. We submit ourselves to Your will and to those whom You have placed in our lives.

We break and renounce all agreements known and unknown made with the spirits of Jezebel, divination, pharmakia, fear, doubt, and unbelief by those in our bloodline. We break and renounce all agreements known and unknown made with the enemy of our souls by those in our bloodline. We destroy every demonic assignment against our lives, our bloodline, and the lives of those with whom we have fellowship.

We decree and declare that the Lord of the Breakthrough will go before us and the Breaker's anointing will rest upon our bloodline. Break through our enemies like the rushing of water. To crossover to the other side, we risk everything, surrender our entire being, and sacrifice all.

We allow the faith of God to arise within us. God bear us up on eagles' wings and uphold us with Your mighty right hand. We will not allow the purpose of God to be aborted. We birth forth the mind and will of God for our bloodline.

Father, give us the grace to move forward. Father, show us the way to go. Strengthen us that we may move forward. We make a decision to move into all that You have for us. We pull down the stronghold of the spirit of fear. Father, You are our history, our present, and our future.

We remember all that You have done for us and how You have delivered us in times past. You always cause us to triumph. Father, we refuse to listen to any demonic spirit or stronghold that says we cannot enter into our destiny. We resist the suggestions of the enemy and give our attention to You alone.

Father, give us a fresh wind of prophetic revelation. Father, cause us to walk in Your favor that we may enter Your courts. Through Your favor and intimate fellowship, cause us to save our nation. Whatever we need to change, Father, cause us to see and hear You clearly. We surrender completely to the work of the Holy Spirit by Your grace in Jesus' name. Amen!

Scripture References: *2 Chronicles 14:11; 2 Samuel 5:20; 2 Corinthians 10:3-6; 2 Corinthians 12:9*

PRAYERS TO FRAME YOUR PROPHETIC DESTINY
WORKSHEET

(This may be used as a guide to help you begin to frame your destiny.)

My personal Conversation with the Father regarding:

___

Discover what the Word of God says about:

___

Search out and write down the verses in the Bible that mention the word(s), phrase(s), or concept(s):

___

___

How are these word(s), phrase(s), or concept(s) applicable to you, your family, your church, your community, or your nation?

___

___

What do you want to say to the Father about what He has said?

___

___

Take a moment to meditate on the Word(s) that seem more pronounced to you as you read what God has to say. After meditating on what He has said, what do you hear the Holy Spirit speaking to your Heart? Take the Scriptures you found, along with what the Holy Spirit is speaking to your heart, and use them to change and frame your destiny:

___

___

___

Persistent Prayer

I dedicate this prayer to those who have family members in need of deliverance from all forms of addiction. May God grant you victory through the power that rests in the Name and Blood of Jesus the Christ. As you war on the behalf of your loved ones, may God cause you to stand clothed in the full armor of God. Be comforted in these Words that the Lord spoke to me when he inspired me to write this decree: **"I am only a mystery to those who do not seek. Yet, I am revealed to those who come, seek, knock, and ask, says the Lord. Keep seeking. Keep knocking. Keep asking."**

> *Again I say unto you, that if two of you shall agree on earth as touching any thing that they shall ask, it shall be done for them of my Father which is in heaven (Matthew 18:19).*

> *And he spake a parable unto them to this end, that men ought always to pray, and not to faint; Saying, There was in a city a judge, which feared not God, neither regarded man: And there was a widow in that city; and she came unto him, saying, Avenge me of mine adversary. And he would not for a while: but afterward he said within himself, Though I fear not God, nor regard man; Yet because this widow troubleth me, I will avenge her, lest by her continual*

coming she weary me. And the Lord said, Hear what the unjust judge saith. And shall not God avenge his own elect, which cry day and night unto him, though he bear long with them? I tell you that he will avenge them speedily. Nevertheless when the Son of man cometh, shall he find faith on the earth? (Luke 18:1-8)

The Deliverance Decree

We come to seek, knock, and ask on behalf of (_____). Reveal yourself to (him/her). We call forth (_____'s) God-ordained, manifest destiny to come forth NOW!

May the words of this decree be so clearly heard and penetrate the spirit realm that even (_____) would begin to hear the very words declared over (his/her) life. May these words begin to rise up in (his/her) own spirit in Jesus' name.

(_____), come forth out of your spiritual darkness. Show yourself, and come into the light of the Son of Righteousness so your pastures are not in deserts or barren land, but on the grass-covered hills.

We declare that you are free from your underground prison cell. We command the strong man to release (_____) from (his/her) prison cell. We command (_____) to arise and come forth. We speak to (his/her) spirit man a word of complete and total deliverance. We cast out the spirits of rejection, abandonment, and every unclean spirit. We command every evil spirit to loose (him/her) and let (him/her) go free. We break the bands of wickedness. We undo the heavy burden. We decree and declare (_____) is free from every oppressive spirit. We command every spirit, unlike God, to manifest and go in the name of Jesus the Christ. We break every generational curse known and unknown over (_____'s) life, in Jesus' name. We make war in the heavenlies on behalf of (_____). Father, send forth Your warring angels to fight on (his/her) behalf for (his/her) deliverance. May the words, "You are delivered" begin to ring in (_____'s) spirit. Lord, visit (him/her)!

(_____), we command you to present yourself to the Lord that He may Shepherd you. (_____), associate yourself with Christ, and He will give you direction, change your course of life and form your character. Father, we stand in the gap and make up the hedge, so that there is no gap between YOU and (_____).

Father, we cry out on behalf of (_____) that You would tend to (him/her), and set (him/her) on a smooth high hill that (he/she) may see clearly. Lord, satisfy (him/her) with good things. Cause (his/her) desire to be upon You. Water every dry and barren place in (his/her) life. May (he/she) experience Your deep, compassionate, tender affection. Father, water (his/her) soul, and pour Your healing waters on every wound, so (he/she) is never found thirsty or lacking again.

Father, grant (him/her) favor, life, and visit (him/her) to preserve (his/her) life. We cancel the plan and plot of the enemy to destroy (his/her) life before YOUR appointed time.

Father, lead (him/her) to YOUR fountain that (he/she) may drink, and experience a place of abundance leading to refreshment. We decree and declare YOU will lead (him/her) out, and give (him/her) rest. For in YOUR presence, YOU will guard, protect, and sustain (his/her) life. We seal our prayers with the precious blood of CHRIST:

> Who is inclined to goodness,

> Who is the very essence of God,
> Who is the perfect expression of truth,
> You are relentless.
> YOU are the ONE on whom we can rely,
> YOU fulfill the meaning of YOUR name,
> YOU cannot lie,
> YOU are marked by truth,
> YOU act in complete conformity to the will and purposes of God.

Father, we acknowledge Your sovereign hand in the life of (_____) and trust that You hear us. If You hear us, we know that You will answer us. In Jesus' name, so be it!

Scripture Reference: *Isaiah 49*

PRAYERS TO FRAME YOUR PROPHETIC DESTINY
WORKSHEET

(This may be used as a guide to help you begin to frame your destiny.)

My personal Conversation with the Father regarding:

_____

Discover what the Word of God says about:

_____

Search out and write down the verses in the Bible that mention the word(s), phrase(s), or concept(s):

_____

_____

How are these word(s), phrase(s), or concept(s) applicable to you, your family, your church, your community, or your nation?

_____

_____

What do you want to say to the Father about what He has said?

_____

_____

Take a moment to meditate on the Word(s) that seem more pronounced to you as you read what God has to say. After meditating on what He has said, what do you hear the Holy Spirit speaking to your Heart? Take the Scriptures you found, along with what the Holy Spirit is speaking to your heart, and use them to change and frame your destiny:

_____

_____

_____

Isaiah 42

You will bring forth justice, and reveal truth in our nation and in our region. You will not fail to establish justice in our coastal region. We wait expectantly on Your just ruling and direction for our nation and region. You are the Lord of creation. You stretched forth the Heavens and expanded the Earth. You give breath and spirit. You are Adonai; our Lord and Master. That is Your Name. We will not give Your glory to another nor Your praise to others or to things. You alone deserve our worship.

Father, as a part of our new Covenant, You have given us Christ. He sealed it with His own precious blood. Therefore, we call forth the blind, those in invisible dungeons, and those who sit in darkness from their iniquitous prisons into a new life in Christ Jesus.

We call forth the former things and declare new things. Before they spring forth, You will tell us. We sing unto You a new song and Your praise from our region. We sing a song in our region that has never been heard. The song that You give us will pierce the darkness and open the windows, Heavens, gates, and portals for the King of glory to come in perpetually.

Father, we lift up our voices from the wilderness, and we shout from the mountain tops of our region. Be exalted oh King of Glory, oh Lord of the Breakthrough. Cause us to pass through. We give glory to the KING OF KINGS and the LORD OF LORDS, and declare Your praise in our region. Be magnified.

Oh Lord of Hosts, go forth like a mighty man, and rise up in Your zealous indignation and vengeance like a warrior. Cry and shout aloud, and do mightily against our enemies in this region. Oh Lord of Hosts, hold not Thy peace or aid from our region be not still nor restrain Yourself, for we rest and trust in Your name.

Oh Lord of Hosts, waste the mountains and hills, dry up the herbage, rivers, and pools of the enemy in our region. Oh Lord of Hosts, bring the blind by a way they know not; lead them in paths they have not known. Make the darkness into light before them, and make uneven places into a plain. Do not leave them forsaken in our region. Put those in our region to shame and turn them back who will not trust in You.

Father, we repent on behalf of our region. We stand in the gap, and we make up the hedge. Do not destroy us; have mercy on our region as You show mercy to thousands of generations. Your covenant You will not alter. Remember Your covenant, and Your sure mercies that You spoke to Your servant David. Do not pass us by, but cause us to pass through the gates that we may enter into Your plan, will, and purpose.

Let us hear Your voice. Speak and roll Your voice like thunder in our region. Speak with a full, loud voice so that those in our region may turn and hear You. Let the report and rumor of the Lord be widely spread in our region.

Lord, speak with a powerful noise; like that of many waters. Let there be a sound as an abundance of rain; like the sound of many rushing waters. Speak Lord! Speak in our region. For at Your

Word, there is a breaking, there is a flowing, there is a birthing, there is release, and there is breath for healing and restoration.

BREATHE LORD. BREATHE ON OUR REGION. WE PROPHESY TO THE FOUR WINDS, THE NORTH, SOUTH, EAST, AND THE WEST WINDS: "BRING FORTH THE WIND OF THE LORD THAT OUR REGION MAY KNOW AND UNDERSTAND THAT OUR GOD IS LORD OF ALL CREATION."

We seal this prayer in the name of Jesus the Christ. Amen!

Scripture Reference: *Isaiah 42*

PRAYERS TO FRAME YOUR PROPHETIC DESTINY
WORKSHEET

(This may be used as a guide to help you begin to frame your destiny.)

My personal Conversation with the Father regarding:

_____

Discover what the Word of God says about:

_____

Search out and write down the verses in the Bible that mention the word(s), phrase(s), or concept(s):

_____
_____

How are these word(s), phrase(s), or concept(s) applicable to you, your family, your church, your community, or your nation?

_____
_____

What do you want to say to the Father about what He has said?

_____
_____

Take a moment to meditate on the Word(s) that seem more pronounced to you as you read what God has to say. After meditating on what He has said, what do you hear the Holy Spirit speaking to your Heart? Take the Scriptures you found, along with what the Holy Spirit is speaking to your heart, and use them to change and frame your destiny:

_____
_____
_____

Standing in the Gap

Father, we stand in the gap for our nation, our country, our state, our region, our city, our community, our church, and our family. Father, forgive us for our attitudes of pride and self-sufficiency. Father, we acknowledge Your sovereignty in the affairs of this nation. On behalf of our nation, I acknowledge that there are divine spiritual laws at work and hereby submit to them that we may alter the impending judgment and bring about true peace and prosperity in Christ Jesus.

Father, we humble ourselves on behalf of this nation, our country, our state, our region, our city, our community, our church, and our family. For You said:

> *If my people, which are called by my name, shall humble themselves, and pray, and seek my face, and turn from their wicked ways; then will I hear from heaven, and will forgive their sin, and will heal their land (2 Chronicles 7:14).*

Father, You said that You looked for someone to stand in the gap and to make up the hedge. Father, here we are standing in the gap. Father, show us the gate of heaven that the Heavens may open once again upon this nation.

As Your voice in the Earth and with the authority we have in the name of Jesus Christ, we declare that mass salvations, deliverances, and healings will occur in our nation in our time. Lord, we know You will not condemn us with the world. For Your Name's sake, show us Your glory. Send revival. Open the Heavens.

Father, we stand firm and refuse to compromise our faith. This nation will not be overcome by evil, but we overcome evil with good. We know You work all things after the counsel of Your will, therefore, we humbly submit to Your will. We acknowledge Christ as the Supreme Ruler, and we pray:

> *That the God of our Lord Jesus Christ, the Father of glory, may give unto us the spirit of wisdom and revelation in the knowledge of him:*
>
> *The eyes of our understanding being enlightened; that we may know what is the hope of his calling, and what the riches of the glory of his inheritance in the saints,*
>
> *And what [is] the exceeding greatness of his power to us-ward who believe, according to the working of his mighty power,*
>
> *Which he wrought in Christ, when he raised him from the dead, and set [him] at his own right hand in the heavenly [places],*
>
> *Far above all principality, and power, and might, and dominion, and every name that is named, not only in this world, but also in that which is to come:*

And hath put all [things] under his feet, and gave him [to be] the head over all [things] to the church, Which is his body, the fullness of him that filleth all in all (Ephesians 1:17-23).

We seal this prayer in the name of Jesus the Christ. Amen!

Scripture References: *Ezekiel 22:30; 2 Chronicles 7:14-15; Ephesians 1:17-23*

PRAYERS TO FRAME YOUR PROPHETIC DESTINY
WORKSHEET

(This may be used as a guide to help you begin to frame your destiny.)

My personal Conversation with the Father regarding:

_____

Discover what the Word of God says about:

_____

Search out and write down the verses in the Bible that mention the word(s), phrase(s), or concept(s):

_____

_____

How are these word(s), phrase(s), or concept(s) applicable to you, your family, your church, your community, or your nation?

_____

_____

What do you want to say to the Father about what He has said?

_____

_____

Take a moment to meditate on the Word(s) that seem more pronounced to you as you read what God has to say. After meditating on what He has said, what do you hear the Holy Spirit speaking to your Heart? Take the Scriptures you found, along with what the Holy Spirit is speaking to your heart, and use them to change and frame your destiny:

_____

_____

_____

Restoring the Foundations of Righteousness

Father, we ask You to forgive the people in our region for breaking covenant with You. We stand in the gap as intercessors and make up the spiritual hedges. We lay hold to the promise of our father Abraham and possess the gates of our enemies, which are Your enemies. We declare that satan would no longer have a safe place to hide in our region. You are the Supreme Watchman and You see all things. We decree and declare that through worship, intercession, fasting, and the prayers of the ministers that weep between the porch and the altar, our region will once again be recaptured for the Lord.

We close the door to demonic influences and open the gate to the move of the Holy Spirit. Lord, use us as a catalyst for revival. Give us a burden to win souls, and see the lost truly converted. God create in us a hunger and thirst that only You can satisfy. Give us pure hearts that we may see You.

Lord, keep us, and bear in mind Your covenant that was established through the blood of Jesus Christ. Allow our generation to restore the land and to reassign its deserted godly legacies. Give us an overwhelming desire to dig the wells of revival. Father, in spite of the world's drought, cause us to sow in the land in which You have planted us, that we may reap a hundred-fold as Jacob did. Father, allow us to rebuild the ancient ruins and raise up the age-old foundations that we may be called the repairers of the breach and the restorer of the streets to dwell in. We decree and declare that the wicked will not remain over the land allotted to the righteous.

Father, we ask for an outpouring of grace, mercy, and fire. Send Your Holy Spirit to cleanse us, break us, and humble us, so that true spiritual revival can come to cover our nation, causing a turning back to God. We ask that the destiny of our region and our nation not be aborted. Visit and abide with us, filling our homes, our churches, and our communities with Your glory. DO NOT PASS US BY!

We ask for a restoration of the foundations of righteousness for our region and nation. We oppose the spirit of wickedness and all other demonic strongholds in our region and nation. Father, open our eyes to the spiritual strongholds in our region and in our nation, so that we may stand clothed in the full armor of God to dismantle them. We build a spiritual, prophetic hedge around our region and our nation with the Word of God and the Blood of Christ.

We seal this prayer in the name of Jesus the Christ. Amen!

Scripture References*: Genesis 22:17; Job 34:21-22; Joel 2:17; Matthew 5:6; Genesis 26:12; Isaiah 58:12*

Prayers to Frame your Prophetic Destiny
Worksheet

(This may be used as a guide to help you begin to frame your destiny.)

My personal Conversation with the Father regarding:

_____

Discover what the Word of God says about:

_____
_____

Search out and write down the verses in the Bible that mention the word(s), phrase(s), or concept(s):

_____
_____
_____

How are these word(s), phrase(s), or concept(s) applicable to you, your family, your church, your community, or your nation?

_____
_____
_____
_____
_____
_____
_____

What do you want to say to the Father about what He has said?

_____
_____
_____

Take a moment to meditate on the Word(s) that seem more pronounced to you as you read what God has to say. After meditating on what He has said, what do you hear the Holy Spirit speaking to your Heart? Take the Scriptures you found, along with what the Holy Spirit is speaking to your heart, and use them to change and frame your destiny:

_____
_____
_____
_____
_____
_____
_____
_____
_____
_____
_____
_____
_____
_____
_____
_____
_____
_____

Digging the Wells of Revival

Father, as we continue in our chronos times of prayer, cause us to recognize our kairos–divinely appointed moments. Let us remain persistent in our intimacy with You. We seek for understanding to know Your mind, will, timing, and purpose. We make ourselves available to be used as spiritual wombs that You may birth Your purpose in the Earth. Cause us to sow in tears that we may reap a harvest. Cause us to overthrow principalities and to shut the mouths of lions. Give us tears of repentance, compassion, and grace that we may change the destiny of nations.

Father, cause us to become a well-watered garden, like a spring whose waters never fail. Bring about old-time revival of sinners converted, the sick healed, creative miracles performed, and the power of God demonstrated as You will. Let us experience the impossible and see the invisible. Father, we prepare ourselves to receive Your revelation.

Father, until the curse of evil is removed from our land and the wells of revival are dug again, we commit to cycles of fasting and praying, as You lead, in Jesus' name. Amen!

Scripture References: *Colossians 4:2; Psalms 126:5; Ephesians 6:12*

PRAYERS TO FRAME YOUR PROPHETIC DESTINY
WORKSHEET

(This may be used as a guide to help you begin to frame your destiny.)

My personal Conversation with the Father regarding:

_____

Discover what the Word of God says about:

_____

Search out and write down the verses in the Bible that mention the word(s), phrase(s), or concept(s):

_____

_____

How are these word(s), phrase(s), or concept(s) applicable to you, your family, your church, your community, or your nation?

_____

_____

What do you want to say to the Father about what He has said?

_____

Take a moment to meditate on the Word(s) that seem more pronounced to you as you read what God has to say. After meditating on what He has said, what do you hear the Holy Spirit speaking to your Heart? Take the Scriptures you found, along with what the Holy Spirit is speaking to your heart, and use them to change and frame your destiny:

_____

_____

_____

A Watchman's Prayer for the Ministry

Father, I thank You that You have raised us up together in heavenly places in Christ Jesus; far above principalities, powers, and rulers of darkness, and spiritual wickedness in high places. From this position in Christ, we use the weapons of our warfare to regulate the course You have given us. We decree and declare the mind, will, and purpose of Christ are operative in our ministry and in our lives. Your Kingdom come, Your will be done in Earth as it is in Heaven.

Father, as You did for the three Hebrew children impart to us knowledge, skillfulness, and wisdom, by Your Holy Spirit. We thank You for Your grace and favor in our ministry and lives.

We decree and declare that we will preserve, change, and protect the ministry You have assigned us to watch over through Apostolic and prophetic intercession. Father, through the gifts of the Holy Spirit, allow us to expose the strategies of the enemy before they become evident. We build a hedge of protection through our Spirit-led intercession.

We decree and declare that our eyes are trained by Your Spirit to discern the spiritual warfare. We decree and declare that we are alert to what is good, what is evil, and to every temptation. We dismantle and frustrate the methodical plans of the enemy against this ministry in Jesus' name. Deliver this ministry from evil. Lord, open our eyes, and let deception be far from this ministry.

Father, position others who will stand alongside Your watchmen. Lord, grant wisdom, and insight as we stand on our ward. We decree and declare that the watchmen in the ministry are thriving on every watch through prophetic insight.

We rebuke every vicious rumor, device, and accusatory conversation against our Pastor, his family, and the ministry. Father, we ask for the gift of discerning of spirits to be dynamic in our lives to see the snakes and wolves in sheep clothing.

We bind the voice of the enemy, and we bind every spirit that would come to vex us in the areas You have called us to watch over. We decree and declare that every demonic influence in the ministry is revealed, exposed, and expelled. We release the voice of Your trumpet over the ministry.

We refuse to come off our watch. Let us perceive the times, seasons, and pray as led by Your Spirit. Father, by your Spirit, instruct us in wisdom and integrity. Father, give us the ability to distinguish Your divine will.

Speak to us in visions, words of knowledge, and dreams. Lord, teach us how to regulate the course of events in the spiritual realm by Your Spirit. Let the light of Jesus Christ within us illuminate the dark places, and light our pathway. We thank You for the spirit of wisdom, the spirit of understanding, the spirit of revelation knowledge, and spiritual insight to the mysteries of the Kingdom of Heaven.

We activate the Issachar anointing to understand the times, seasons, and how to respond on behalf of those You have given us watch over. We decree and declare that we are empowered to build up, establish, and uplift those for whom we watch, according to Your divine purposes. In those times when You have us stand as intercessors, we commit to watch over other watchmen in Your house. Father, continually raise up intercessors among us that understand Your heart.

Father, let no false words come from our mouths. I thank You for accuracy in the prophetic. We decree and declare that our ears are open to hear Your voice and obey promptly the entire scroll of Your Word. Search us with the light of Your Word and purify our every motive and intent. Father, may we be sensitive to the Holy Spirit's training and discipline.

Father, refine us that we may yield a fruitful field. Deepen our relationship and intensify our communion with You. May we work hand-in-hand with other watchmen, intercessors, gatekeepers, interpreters of dreams and visions, and administrators of the Spirit of God.

We bind ourselves to Your covenant promises. Father, give us clear insight regarding what is bound, closed, loosed, and opened by the spirit of wisdom and revelation, so we operate in harmony with Your will, in Jesus' name. Amen!

Scripture References: *Ephesians 2:6; Ephesians 1:17-21; Luke 11:2; 1 Chronicles 12:32; Psalm 139:23*

Prayers to Frame your Prophetic Destiny
Worksheet

(This may be used as a guide to help you begin to frame your destiny.)

My personal Conversation with the Father regarding:

_____

Discover what the Word of God says about:

_____

Search out and write down the verses in the Bible that mention the word(s), phrase(s), or concept(s):

_____

_____

How are these word(s), phrase(s), or concept(s) applicable to you, your family, your church, your community, or your nation?

_____

_____

What do you want to say to the Father about what He has said?

_____

_____

Take a moment to meditate on the Word(s) that seem more pronounced to you as you read what God has to say. After meditating on what He has said, what do you hear the Holy Spirit speaking to your Heart? Take the Scriptures you found, along with what the Holy Spirit is speaking to your heart, and use them to change and frame your destiny:

_____

_____

_____

A Watchman's Prayers for Pastors

From the man of God and his family, we cut off and draw away every ungodly tie. We pluck up its roots and strip off its fruit and declare that all its fresh sprouting leaves will wither, so that it is incapable of producing. We decree and declare that the Lord of Hosts will bring down the high tree and exalt the low tree. We declare that You will dry up the false green tree that was planted and allowed to thrive and will cause the faithful dry tree to flourish. We decree and declare that You will do it by Your might and Your power.

We castrate, tear up, and tear off every root sown among the man of God and his family. We separate and draw away every enslaving yoke and every binding chain. We break every band of restraint asunder and cast the enemy's cords of control from them into a dark dry place. Bring them out of darkness and every shadow of death. We break apart every bond holding them.

Lord, pull out every rebellious one that has been planted. Like a sheep for the slaughter, devote and prepare them for the day of slaughter. We draw away from and cut off every attachment of the enemy that has been sown among the man of God and his family. We send out ambushments against the enemy.

We tear away and break every cord of the enemy that has been wrapped around the man of God and his family. Utter Your voice and roar like a lion before their enemy so the Heavens, and the Earth will know they are called by Your name. We cover the secret of their strength and the area of their weakness with the blood of Christ, that it may not be known to the enemy that lies in wait.

We decree and declare that his dwelling is a place of quietness, a tent that will not be taken down. We declare that not one of his stakes that You have established will ever be pulled up, nor will the cords that You have set in place be broken.

We declare that the enemy will not be able to frustrate the plans and purposes of God for the man of God's life. We decree and declare that every godly desire and possession of his heart is established.

Father, we stand by the roads to look and ask for eternal paths where the good old way is, and decree and declare that the man of God will walk in it and find rest. May he hear and obey Your trumpet, in Jesus' name. Amen.

Scripture References*: Ezekiel 17:9,24; Psalm 2:3; Jeremiah 12:3; Isaiah 33:20; Jeremiah 6:16-17, 27*

Conversations of a Watchman

PRAYERS TO FRAME YOUR PROPHETIC DESTINY

WORKSHEET

(This may be used as a guide to help you begin to frame your destiny.)

My personal Conversation with the Father regarding:

_____

Discover what the Word of God says about:

_____

_____

Search out and write down the verses in the Bible that mention the word(s), phrase(s), or concept(s):

_____

_____

_____

How are these word(s), phrase(s), or concept(s) applicable to you, your family, your church, your community, or your nation?

_____

_____

_____

_____

_____

_____

_____

What do you want to say to the Father about what He has said?

_____
_____
_____

Take a moment to meditate on the Word(s) that seem more pronounced to you as you read what God has to say. After meditating on what He has said, what do you hear the Holy Spirit speaking to your Heart? Take the Scriptures you found, along with what the Holy Spirit is speaking to your heart, and use them to change and frame your destiny:

_____
_____
_____
_____
_____
_____
_____
_____
_____
_____
_____
_____
_____
_____
_____
_____
_____

The Enemies Strategy – Conspiracies

Oftentimes in different facets of our lives, we find ourselves surrounded by an invisible force field that seems impenetrable. At other times, the people we work with cannot work together in harmony for no apparent reason or for some insignificant reason. In those times, it is vital to seek direction from God and gain spiritual insight and strategy from the Holy Spirit.

Oftentimes the enemy uses spiritual strategies to distract, detain, and ultimately destroy the divine purposes of God for our lives. One of his tactics is to use conspiracies. A conspiracy is a plot, plan, or scheme operating in a covert manner producing division and schism between individuals, groups, ministries, nations, etc.

After reading *2 Chronicles 24* and seeing how conspiracy led to the death of the priest Zechariah, and the execution of God's judgment against Judah and Jerusalem, this prayer was inspired by the Holy Spirit to pray over the ministry where I serve.

A Prayer against Conspiracies

We decree and declare that every conspiracy, coalition, collusion and secret alliance, known and unknown, meant to bring about division, schism and separation, be revealed and severed.

We decree and declare that every plot, covert scheme meant for our destruction be brought to naught.

We decree and declare that every secret agreement containing a harmful objective be broken by the power that is in the name of Jesus the Christ.

We decree and declare that every entity in the natural and spiritual realms operating with deceitful and treacherous intentions, be exposed, uprooted, and expelled.

We disassociate ourselves, our loved ones, our ministry, our pastor, our pastor's wife, our pastor's children, every intercessor, the leadership, the Worship Arts Ministry, and the Production Ministry, from all unlawful unions, alliances, affiliations, integrations, and secret understandings. Instead, we decree and declare that those who are willing to walk in cooperation and collaboration be drawn together to fulfill the divine purpose and destiny of God for our lives and for the ministry.

We sever every clique, connection, faction, federation, guild, partnership, and syndicate that has gathered together against us, our loved ones, our ministry, our pastor and his family, every Intercessor, the Worship Arts Ministry, and the Production Ministry.

We declare *Isaiah 54:17*

No weapon that is formed against thee shall prosper; and every tongue [that] shall rise against thee in judgment thou shalt condemn. This [is] the heritage of the servants of the LORD, and their righteousness [is] of me, saith the LORD.

We seal this prayer in the name of Jesus the Christ. Amen!

Scripture Reference: *2 Chronicles 24*

PRAYERS TO FRAME YOUR PROPHETIC DESTINY
WORKSHEET

(This may be used as a guide to help you begin to frame your destiny.)

My personal Conversation with the Father regarding:

Discover what the Word of God says about:

Search out and write down the verses in the Bible that mention the word(s), phrase(s), or concept(s):

How are these word(s), phrase(s), or concept(s) applicable to you, your family, your church, your community, or your nation?

What do you want to say to the Father about what He has said?

Take a moment to meditate on the Word(s) that seem more pronounced to you as you read what God has to say. After meditating on what He has said, what do you hear the Holy Spirit speaking to your Heart? Take the Scriptures you found, along with what the Holy Spirit is speaking to your heart, and use them to change and frame your destiny:

Fan the Flames to Harvest the Souls

Father, make Your angels winds and Your ministers to be flames of fire, so a Kingdom harvest will be gathered by Your might and by Your power.

We come against those things that would undermine the full release of Your Spirit. We cast down human striving, selfish ambition, and pride, in Jesus' name. Father, we submit ourselves in the spirit of humility and resist the devil. We serve and cooperate with You because of Your loyal love toward us.

We eradicate all carnality, false ambition, and deception, in the name of Jesus. Purify us that we may sustain Your presence and be loyal stewards of Your glory. Use us to restore the Tabernacle of David, to close up the breaches, and bring in the end time harvest of souls for Your kingdom, in Jesus' name. Amen!

Scripture References: *Psalm 104:4; Hebrews 1:7 (Amplified); Amos 9:11*

PRAYERS TO FRAME YOUR PROPHETIC DESTINY
WORKSHEET

(This may be used as a guide to help you begin to frame your destiny.)

My personal Conversation with the Father regarding:

_____

Discover what the Word of God says about:

_____

Search out and write down the verses in the Bible that mention the word(s), phrase(s), or concept(s):

_____

How are these word(s), phrase(s), or concept(s) applicable to you, your family, your church, your community, or your nation?

_____

What do you want to say to the Father about what He has said?

_____

Take a moment to meditate on the Word(s) that seem more pronounced to you as you read what God has to say. After meditating on what He has said, what do you hear the Holy Spirit speaking to your Heart? Take the Scriptures you found, along with what the Holy Spirit is speaking to your heart, and use them to change and frame your destiny:

_____

_____

About the Author

K. E. ALLEN has proven to be an incredible, spiritual force in the Kingdom of God by displaying a God given indomitable spirit to change atmospheres and environments. Through the extraordinary gift of intercession and pure worship, she has become a spiritual weapon in the hand of the Lord whose knowledge is relevant for the church today. She is a dynamic leader, extravagant worshiper and prophetic intercessor whose worship has become a definitive lifestyle that penetrates and permeates every facet of her life and the lives of those she touches.

Karla is a leader to leaders and lives a life of committed consistent intercession, giving selflessly of herself in her prayer closet. For over 25 years, as a student and teacher of the Word and woman of faith, she implements the truth of the Bible through the dynamics of intercession and worship that releases a tangible anointing. Knowing firsthand the transformative power of God in her own life, she is determined to see others healed, delivered and set free. Karla will stop at nothing to see God move in the lives of His people!

www.ingramcontent.com/pod-product-compliance
Lightning Source LLC
LaVergne TN
LVHW051558070426
835507LV00021B/2652